Australia

Bill Coppell has enjoyed a long and distinguished career as an educator. After working as a primary school teacher in New Zealand and the Pacific Islands, he became Vice-principal of Nasinu Teacher's College in Fiji, and later Deputy-director of Education in the Cook Islands. From 1969 to 1989, he was a senior lecturer in Education at Macquarie University, with particular interests in Aboriginal and migrant education. Now living in Canberra, Bill Coppell was a visiting fellow at the Australian National University. He is a registered book indexer, and has produced specialised bibliographies about the Pacific Islands. A keen sportsman who, at various times, has enjoyed rugby union, softball, yachting and golf, he now restricts himself to the occasional game of bowls.

To Merle

For providing inspiration,
help and understanding

AUSTRALIA
in facts and figures

BILL COPPELL

Penguin Books

I wish to thank the many Commonwealth departments and other organisations which have so readily provided me with the information upon which much of the material in this book is based. Special thanks go to the staff of the Library of the Australian Bureau of Statistics.

Penguin Books Australia Ltd
487 Maroondah Highway, PO Box 257
Ringwood, Victoria 3134, Australia
Penguin Books Ltd
Harmondsworth, Middlesex, England
Penguin Putnam Inc.
375 Hudson Street, New York, New York 10014, USA
Penguin Books Canada Limited
10 Alcorn Avenue, Toronto, Ontario, Canada M4V 3B2
Penguin Books (NZ) Ltd
Cnr Rosedale and Airborne Roads, Albany, Auckland, New Zealand
Penguin Books (South Africa) (Pty) Ltd
4 Pallinghurst Road, Parktown 2193, South Africa

First published as *Australia in Figures* by Penguin Books Australia 1974
Reprinted in revised editions 1981, 1994
This fully revised edition published by Penguin Books Australia Ltd 1999

10 9 8 7 6 5 4 3 2 1

Copyright © Bill Coppell 1974, 1981, 1994, 1999

All rights reserved. Without limiting the rights under copyright reserved above, no part of this publication may be reproduced, stored in or introduced into a retrieval system, or transmitted, in any form or by any means (electronic, mechanical, photocopying, recording or otherwise), without the prior written permission of both the copyright owner and the above publisher of this book.

Designed by Lynn Twelftree
Typeset in Novarese by Post Pre-press Group, Brisbane
Printed in Australia by Australian Print Group, Maryborough, Victoria

National Library of Australia
Cataloguing-in-Publication data:

Coppell, W. G. (William George).
  Australia in facts and figures.
  Rev. ed.
  Includes index.

ISBN 0 14 027138 4.

1. Australia. 2. Australia – Statistics. I. Title.

319.4

CONTENTS

Introduction	vii
Abbreviations	ix

The Land — 1
Geography	2
Climate	8
Flora and fauna	14
Register of the National Estate	30
Land utilisation	33
The environment	33

The People — 39
An overview	40
Births	53
Deaths	58
Marriage	65
The family	70
Religion	77
Languages	79
Housing	82
Health	87
Social security and welfare	101
Food and nutrition	105
Education and training	108

Labour	120
The criminal justice system	132
Entertainment and recreation	145

The Government — 157
Structure of government	158
Defence	169

The Economy — 177
Economic overview	178

Trade and Industry — 187
An overview	188
Primary industries	188
Science and technology	202
Energy	204
Transport	207
Tourism and the hospitality industry	218
Mining and minerals	222
Construction industry	225

Communications — 227
The media	228
Communication services	231

Index	236

INTRODUCTION

This edition of *Australia in Facts and Figures*, like the previous ones, aims to meet the needs of all those who are interested in the development of Australian society. Many readers seek statistical information in an easily understandable form, which is not always available in the tables of government and other official publications. I hope that information is present here.

At all times this edition avoids setting out information that is static, focusing only upon a single moment in time. The book's emphasis is upon changes which have occurred over time, or upon differences which exist between the states of the Commonwealth, or between Australia and other countries with similar social or economic structures.

This emphasis is supported by commentaries which may define terms, supply information of historical significance, or set out issues of contemporary relevance. These commentaries are supported by graphic presentations that display various aspects of the selected topics. The scales used and the limitations placed upon precise accuracy are such that readers should not try to ascertain specific values, but should make generalised estimates using the key values included in the graphic displays.

In a number of instances an historical perspective is given to the broad topics selected by making reference to early

Australian records, some of which refer to colonial times. Bringing together statistical information from a number of sources in order to make comparisons is not always satisfactory. Differences in the refinement of data collection and the use of varying reference points may make such comparisons unreliable. Care has been taken to ensure that historical comparisons have been made only where there is a high degree of compatability of data.

It is conceded that a publication such as this suffers from the time-lag between the collection of data and the publication of that data in its final form. As a result, some of the material here is necessarily some years in arrears. Where international comparisons are made, every effort has been taken to bring closely timed data together, in order to ensure that this exercise is valid.

ABBREVIATIONS

ABS	Australian Bureau of Statistics	**ML**	megalitre
ACT	Australian Capital Territory	**mm**	millimetre
bn	billion	**Mt**	megatonne
E	East	**MW**	megawatt
GDP	gross domestic product	**N**	North
GNP	gross national product	**NSW**	New South Wales
ha	hectare	**NT**	Northern Territory
kg	kilogram	**OECD**	Organisation for Economic Cooperation and Development
kj	kilojoule		
kL	kilolitre	**pop'n**	population
km	kilometre	**Qld**	Queensland
kt	kilotonne	**S**	South
kW	kilowatt	**SA**	South Australia
L	litre	**Tas.**	Tasmania
LPG	liquified petroleum gas	**t**	tonne
m	metre; million ($)	**Vic.**	Victoria
m²	square metres	**W**	West
m³	cubic metres	**WA**	Western Australia
mL	millilitre		

GEOGRAPHY

Location, land area and features

Australia is surrounded by the Tasman Sea and Pacific Ocean to the east, the Indian Ocean to the west, the Coral Sea, Arafura Sea and Timor Sea to the north and the Southern Ocean and Great Australian Bight to the south. Situated between latitudes 10°41'S (Cape York, Qld) and 43°49'S (South Cape, Tas.) and longitudes 113°9'E (Steep Point, WA) and 153°39'E (Cape Byron, NSW), the mainland measures about 3690 km from its most northerly point (the tip of Cape York) to South Point, Wilsons Promontory (Vic.), its most southerly point. The longitudinal distance of the mainland from east to west is about 4000 km. The land area of 7 682 300 km² is about the same as the USA (excluding Alaska), about 50% larger than Europe (excluding the former USSR) and 32 times greater than the UK. The 250 km of Bass Strait separates the mainland from Tasmania, which measures about 296 km from north to south and 315 km from east to west. There are hundreds of islands in Australian coastal waters, from coral cays to high continental islands. Melville Island (5698 km²), near

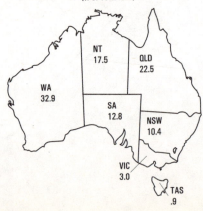

Area of States and Territories
(% of Total Area)

NT 17.5
QLD 22.5
WA 32.9
SA 12.8
NSW 10.4
VIC 3.0
TAS .9

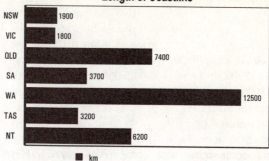

Length of Coastline (km)
- NSW: 1900
- VIC: 1800
- QLD: 7400
- SA: 3700
- WA: 12500
- TAS: 3200
- NT: 6200

Darwin, is the largest island (apart from Tasmania) in Australian waters.
- Mt Kosciuszko (NSW, 2230 m) is the highest point.
- The lowest point is 15 m below sea level at Lake Eyre (SA).
- The continental shelf varies in width between 30 km and 240 km.

Rivers

At 2520 km the Murray River is Australia's longest river, combining with the Darling and Upper Darling rivers to form the Murray–Darling Basin, which extends over 15% of the continent and serves four states and the ACT.
- The Murray River supports about ⅓ of Australia's agricultural production.
- The Murray supports 50% of Australia's sheep and croplands and 25% of beef and dairy herds.
- The Murray contains about 62% of the country's irrigated land, and supplies 50% of SA's water.

More than $200m in production is lost each year through land degradation in cropping and irrigation areas.

Lakes

The largest lakes, Lake Eyre (9500 km^2), Lake Torrens (5900 km^2) and Lake Gairdner (4300 km^2), all in SA, are the drainage areas from the internal rivers and become beds of baked mud in the dry season. Lake St Clair (Tas.) is the deepest lake (168 m) and Lake Argyle (WA) the largest artificial lake (about 700 km^2).

Earthquakes

Compared with other parts of the world, Australia has a relatively low level of earthquake activity. Governor Arthur Phillip recorded a slight shock at Sydney on 22 June 1788. Two recent major earthquakes have caused severe damage and in one case loss of life.

- 1 March 1954: Adelaide. A tremor of 5.6 on the Richter scale caused $71m damage.
- 28 December 1989: Newcastle (NSW). A quake measuring 5.6 on the Richter scale killed 12 people and injured 106. There was moderate to serious damage to 35 000 homes and 3000 other buildings. The total damage bill was conservatively estimated at $1.5bn.

Land degradation

Australian soils are complex and variable and are generally derived from very ancient landscapes. They are among the most mineral-deficient in the world. Prior to European occupation, soil loss was low and the landscape basically stable, but Australian soils are now among the most degraded in developed countries.

- Wind erosion occurs when drier areas lose their plant cover and sandy soils are blown away. This is a serious problem in western NSW, the mallee land of Vic. and the sandy plains of SA and WA.

- As land has been cleared there has often been an increase in the level of groundwater salinity. The groundwater is drawn to the surface by evaporation and capillary action. About 2.2 million ha of productive land has been affected, with an estimated cost of $243m per annum in lost agricultural production. A further 1.4 million ha of land is estimated to be at risk from salination.
- Irrigation salinity and waterlogging are brought about when groundwater levels are raised by factors such as leakage of irrigation channels, inadequate land drainage and overwatering by irrigators.
- Soil-structure decline occurs through overcultivation and continual tramping by stock. Also, the use of heavy equipment when the ground is wet reduces aeration of the soil, a key element in the maintenance of good soil. In terms of income foregone this is the most costly form of land degradation in Australia.
- The loss of native trees and shrubs has been widespread. In many places, vegetation changes have reduced land stability and usefulness. Tree dieback is a significant problem in woodland areas, especially on the NSW tablelands.
- The clearing of vegetation on steeply sloping land has resulted in deep penetration of rainwater into zones of clay, which become unstable when wet, causing landslips.
- Soil acidification results from the continued use of nitrogen-fixing legumes (e.g. subterranean clover) and acidifying fertilisers (e.g. sulphate of ammonia), and can lead to a decline of up to 50% in productivity.

Australian external territories

As well as the mainland territories (NT, ACT), Australia has several offshore territories.

Ashmore Islands and Cartier Islet

Situated 850 km and 790 km respectively west of Darwin in the Indian Ocean, these small, low-lying islands are composed of sand and coral. They were handed to Australia by the UK government in 1933. Ashmore Reef became a national nature reserve in 1983. By agreement between the Australian and Indonesian governments, Indonesian subsistence-level fishermen, who by tradition fished in the territorial waters surrounding the islands, are permitted to have access to them.

Australian Antarctic Territory

On 7 February 1933 an Imperial Order in Council placed under Australian authority all islands and territories (except French Adélie Land) south of 60°S latitude and between 45° and 160°E longitude, covering an area of 6 million km^2. Since 1954, permanent Australian Antarctic stations have been established at Mawson, Davis and Casey. There are also a number of summer bases.

Christmas Island

An isolated island peak up to 360 m above sea level, located at 10°25'S latitude, 105°40'E longitude, Christmas Island is 1312 km from Singapore and 2623 km from Perth. The island was handed over by the UK to Australia on 1 October 1958. In the past the economy was almost entirely dependent on the mining of phosphate rock. Other sources of income are now being developed, particularly fishing, tourism and casino gambling. In 1991 there were 1275 residents, the majority being ethnic Chinese with smaller numbers of Malays and Europeans.

Cocos (Keeling) Islands

Situated 2768 km north-west of Perth and 3685 km west of Darwin at 12°5'S latitude, 96°53'E longitude in the Indian Ocean, this territory comprises two atolls encompassing 27 small coral islands, with a maximum height of 6 m above sea level. It became an Australian territory in 1955 through an agreement with the UK government. In 1991 the population, mainly descended from Malay copra workers, numbered 647. In 1984, in an Act of Self-Determination under United Nations supervision, the residents voted by referendum to be integrated into Australia.

Coral Sea Islands Territory

Situated east of Qld, the territory is located at 156°E longitude and between 12°S and 24°S latitude. Mainly sand and coral, most of the islands are small and have no permanent fresh water. In 1982 the Lifou Reef and Coringa–Herald national nature reserves were proclaimed to protect the flora and fauna.

Heard and McDonald Islands

Heard Island is the largest of a group of islands about 4100 km south-west of Fremantle (WA) and 1500 km north of Antarctica. They were transferred from the UK government to Australian control on 26 December 1947.

Norfolk Island

Norfolk Island is situated 1676 km east of Sydney at 29°3'S latitude and 167°57'E longitude, and is about 3455 ha in area. It was a dependency of NSW until it became a territory of Australia under the *Norfolk Island Act 1913*. In 1991 the population was 2285, of whom 45.95% were descendants of the *Bounty* mutineers. The 1991 census recorded 390 tourists and visitors on the island.

Australian standard times

The meridian 150°E is used for the purposes of standard time in NSW, Vic., Qld, Tas. and the ACT, being 10 hours ahead of Universal Time (UT). For SA and NT the selected meridian is 142°30'E and standard time is 9½ hours ahead of UT. For WA the selected meridian is 120°E and standard time is eight hours ahead of UT. Daylight saving commences and ends at different dates in the various states and territories.

CLIMATE

The climate is basically continental in nature, modified by Australia's insular situation. The continent is relatively dry: 80% has a mean annual rainfall of less than 600 mm, and 50% has less than 300 mm. In general, Australia has a dry environment in terms of the water vapour content or humidity of the air.

The Southern Oscillation Index is a measure of atmospheric pressure of the ocean between the central Pacific and northern Australia. The oscillation is a major determinant of climatic variation. El Niño is marked by extremely dry years and La Niña by extremely wet years.

- Since 1951 there have been seven El Niño-related drought periods in Australia, including that of 1997–98.
- During the year ended June 1997 there was a particularly dramatic change from the weak large-scale climate controls in spring to strong El Niño conditions (after March 1997).
- The northern 'wet' finished abruptly and premature El Niño conditions were established in the autumn of 1997. This was accompanied by a marked warming of the surfaces of the eastern Pacific, with the Southern

Oscillation Index falling from +13.3 in February to −22.4 in May and −24.1 in June.

▶ In May 1998 there was fairly widespread heavy rain and strong indications that the El Niño period was being reversed.

El Niño-related drought periods, 1951–92

Feb. 1951 to Mar. 1952	14 months
Jan. 1965 to Nov. 1965	11 months
Aug. 1968 to Jan. 1970	18 months
Mar. 1972 to Jan. 1973	11 months
Apr. 1982 to Feb. 1983	11 months
Mar. 1991 to Jan. 1992	11 months

The most recent El Niño period began in March–April 1997 and had almost finished by the end of June 1998.

Temperature

Because it is surrounded by oceans and does not have extensive mountain systems, Australia does not experience the extreme minimum temperatures recorded on other continents. Extreme maximum temperatures are experienced, reaching 50°C over inland arid areas. Average annual air temperatures range from 4°C in the alpine region of the south-east to 28°C in the Kimberley (WA) coastal area.

▶ Heat-wave periods, when a number of successive days have temperatures over 40°C, are common in inland regions. In January 1939 a four-day heat wave affected south-eastern Australia, with Adelaide registering a record 47.6°C on 12 January.

▶ Marble Bar (WA) has an average summer maximum temperature of 41°C; the temperature may register over 40°C for several consecutive weeks.

Rainfall

The lowest annual rainfall occurs at Lake Eyre (SA), with an annual mean precipitation of about 100 mm. Tully (Qld) experiences the highest annual rainfall of 4400 mm. On 4 January 1979 Bellenden Ker (Qld) recorded 960 mm in 24 hours, the highest ever Australian 24-hour recording.

Rainfall days are days in which 0.2 mm or more are recorded. There are more than 150 rainfall days per year in Tas., southern Vic., parts of the northern Qld coast and most south-westerly parts of WA. From the north-west of the continent through to Central Australia there are often less than 25 rainfall days in a year.

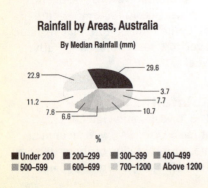

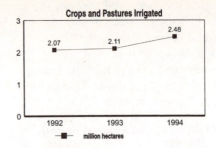

Drought

Droughts are usually assessed in terms of availability of rainfall, and the declaration of drought for an area usually depends on a lack of naturally occurring water for local agrarian industries. Major droughts have extended over several years, e.g. 1864–68, 1880–86, 1911–16, 1918–20 and 1939–45. The 1991–95 drought is estimated to have cost the Australian economy up to $5bn, and $590m in Commonwealth government drought relief.

Flood

The first flood recorded by white

settlers in Australia was in 1789, when the Hawkesbury River, north of Sydney, was 7–12 m above its normal level. Rivers flowing eastward to the sea from the Great Dividing Range, mainly in Qld and NSW, often have sudden and severe flood surges.

- In December 1916, 61 people drowned when a torrential downpour in Claremont (Qld) caused a flood surge to rush through low-lying parts of the town.
- Cyclone Wanda brought flooding to Qld in January 1974, seriously affecting Ipswich and Brisbane. Twelve people drowned, 6700 homes were flooded and the damage was estimated at $300m.

Fog

The foggiest capital city is Canberra, with an annual average of 47 fog days. Brisbane averages 20 fog days, while Darwin averages two.

Snow

Snow covers the Australian Alps above 1500 m from late autumn through to early spring. Tasmania's mountains above 1000 m are often covered with winter snow. There are no permanent snowfields in Australia, although some snow may last through the summer in sheltered ravines on Mt Kosciuszko.

Frost

Frosts can cause serious damage to crops, and specific frost-resistant crops are often grown in affected areas.

- The lowest overnight ground temperatures recorded are −15.1°C at Canberra and −11.0°C at Stanthorpe (Qld).

Wind

Australia is influenced by two wind systems: the south-easterly trade winds blowing on the equatorial side of the mid-latitude anticyclones, and the westerly winds south of the mid-latitude anticyclones in which successive low-pressure systems move eastward over the Southern Ocean. Very strong winds and heavy rainfall over large areas result from active depressions moving westward over the Southern Ocean and from tropical cyclones in the north and north-west.

▶ A gust of 259 km/h was recorded at Mardie (WA) on 19 February 1975.

▶ On 24 December 1974 Cyclone Tracy, the most devastating cyclone in Australian recorded history, struck Darwin. Fifteen lives were lost at sea, with 50 deaths on land. There was catastrophic damage to property and most of the city had to be rebuilt.

Thunder and hail

A thunder-day is a day in which thunder is heard at least once. Darwin experiences about 70 thunder-days annually, compared with less than 10 in southern parts of the continent. Large hailstones more than 10 mm in diameter are sometimes produced by summer thunderstorms in eastern areas of the continent.

Impact of climate change

There are concerns that the depletion of the atmospheric ozone layer and the consequent rise in ocean levels will drastically alter Australian climatic conditions. It is predicted that rainfall will decrease in the Murray–Darling Basin by 40–50%.

Fire

In 1996–97 the NSW Fire Brigade turned out for 99 592 incidents. Of these, 31% were fires and 22% were other emergencies, e.g. over-pressure ruptures of water mains, rescue calls and other hazardous conditions.

◗ The total Australian expenditure for fire services in 1996–97 was about $860m, with the highest expenditure per person being $64 in the NT and the lowest $42 in WA. Funding for fire services is provided by state and territory governments, and by compulsory levies on insurance companies and property owners, user charges and public fundraising.

◗ In NSW in 1996–97 funding for the NSW Fire Brigade totalled $254.8m and for the Rural Fire Service $59.1m.

Bushfires

Bushfires have long been a feature of the Australian environment, as Aboriginal people traditionally used fire to stimulate fresh growth in the bush to attract game. Lightning strikes and spontaneous combustion also cause outbreaks. Many Australian plants are adapted to fire, which can be vital for the germination of seeds.

◗ The Black Friday bushfire in Vic. of 13–15 January 1939 killed 71 people, burnt out an estimated 1.2 million ha of timberland and destroyed 1000 houses and the township of Noojee.

◗ On 7 February 1967 winds of up to 80 km/h swept fires that started on Mount Wellington to within 2 km of the centre of Hobart. In five hours 59 lives were lost and 1300 buildings were destroyed.

◗ In January 1994 bushfires swept NSW: four lives were lost, 600 000 ha of bush was burnt out, 185 houses were destroyed and 12 000 people were cared for at evacuation centres.

Urban fires

The first fire brigades set up in urban areas in Australia were established by insurance companies. In 1848 the Australian

Fire and Life Assurance Company in Sydney formed a 25-man brigade with two stations equipped with two pumping engines.

▶ On 1 December 1864, 50 premises were destroyed in Brisbane when fire engulfed the area bounded by Queen, George, Elizabeth and Albert streets.

▶ A fire in a Melbourne men's convalescent home on 13 August 1966 killed 30 people.

FLORA AND FAUNA

Flora

Because it was isolated from other major land areas for a very long period, Australia developed a flora which included many unique species. Of the approximately 28 000 plant species indigenous to Australia, 85% have not been found elsewhere.

Threatened flora

In its 1995–96 annual report, the Australian Nature Conservation Agency listed 1071 endangered species of vascular plants. The agency spent $5.36m on its Endangered Species Program. Many families, genera and species of plants are now threatened with extinction. Rare or threatened species represent about 17% of the total number of plants native to Australia. Almost 5% (933 species) are considered to be threatened (either endangered or vulnerable) and 97 species (0.5%) are presumed to be extinct.

▶ In August 1994 in a deep, sheltered rainforest gorge in the Wollemi National Park, north of Sydney, a previously unknown species of pine was discovered. Regarded as a living fossil, the Wollemi Pine's closest relatives are fossils from about 100 million years ago.

Forests
Native forests
During the last 200-odd years more than half of Australia's native forests have been cleared, with about 41 million ha of native forest remaining. Rainforests cover less than 10% of the world's land surface but contain 50% of terrestrial plant and animal species. Since the first European settlement, 75% of Australia's rainforests have been destroyed. There are about 1.4 million ha of tropical forest in Australia, confined to Qld, NT and WA.

▸ Native forest makes up 5% of Australia's land area of 768 million ha. Eucalypts are the most dominant native forest species. Seventy-two per cent of the native forest is Crown land, with the remainder having private tenure.

▸ There are four Australian World Heritage areas with significant areas of forest: the Tasmanian wilderness (1.37 million ha), the central eastern rainforest reserves (203 600 ha), the wet tropics area of Qld (890 000 ha) and Fraser Island (166 300 ha).

Plantation forests
There are few conifers in Australia's indigenous forests, and considerable quantities of building timber are now imported. In the latter part of the 19th century pine plantations were established in SA, the state with the smallest area of native forests. At 31 March 1994 there were 1.105 million ha of plantation trees, of which 95% were varieties of exotic pines, with *Pinus radiata* accounting for 86.8%. The remaining plantations were mainly eucalypt species and poplars.

Trees on farms
In the period 1991–94, 45% of farm trees were planted in the pastoral zone, 34% in the wheat/sheep zone and 39% in the high rainfall zone.

Exotic weeds
Many plants have been introduced

to Australia, some for agricultural, horticultural or ornamental purposes and others accidentally. It is estimated that about 800 species are now exotic weeds, and in some places they are more numerous and abundant than native species. Not all these weeds necessarily have undesirable qualities; some may have value as stock fodder.

▶ Bugloss (Paterson's Curse or Salvation Jane), introduced as a garden plant, now smothers wide areas of grazing land from WA to the Riverina (NSW).

▶ The prickly pear, a tall, fast-growing cactus initially used as a hedge plant, had by 1925 affected 26.3 million ha between Mackay (Qld) and Newcastle (NSW): 12.2 million ha were so densely covered as to be useless. Caterpillars of the cactoblastus moth (a native of Argentina and Brazil) were then released and by 1940 the prickly pear had been completely controlled.

▶ Bitou bush is a South African weed which for 40 years has been spreading along the eastern and southern coastline. It reproduces swiftly and can smother almost all other plant forms apart from the biggest trees. Long-term prospects for control appear to be an integration of biological and conventional weed controls, coupled with fire management.

Fauna

Many Australian plants and animals have suffered from the effects of human population growth, habitat destruction, introduced predators and the exploitation of native plants and animals. Introduced grazing mammals, especially sheep and cattle, have restricted the food supplies of many native animals. At the time of the European arrival, Australia's stock of animal species was estimated to be 540 birds, 530 reptiles, 240 marsupials, two monotremes, and two placental mammal groups, bats and the dingo. The monotremes – the echidna and the platypus – are warm-blooded, lay eggs, and suckle their young which are carried in a pouch. Monotremes are unique to Australia.

◗ Over the past 200 years at least 18 species of Australian birds and marsupials have become extinct. The first known species of mammals to have disappeared by 1840 were the lesser stick-nest rat, the long-eared hopping mouse and the Darling Downs hopping mouse.

◗ Some species have been presumed to have become extinct, such as the Tasmanian tiger (thylacine) by 1933, although unconfirmed sightings have occurred in remote areas.

◗ The mountain pygmy possum was rediscovered at the Melbourne University Ski Club lodge at Mt Hotham (Vic.) in 1967.

◗ In its 1995–96 annual report, the Australian Nature Conservation Agency listed 174 endangered or vulnerable species of fauna: 66 mammals, 71 birds, 21 reptiles and 14 freshwater fish species.

Marsupials
Kangaroos

There are 48 species in the Macropodidae family: nine of rat-kangaroo, potoroo and betong, and 39 of kangaroo and wallaby. In 1975 six of the 48 species were listed as extinct, but it is possible that small groups of some of these species may be rediscovered in the future. Twenty-five species are fully protected in all states and territories and 10 are killed for commercial purposes in one or more states. Red, western grey and eastern grey are the species most extensively harvested commercially. In 1995, 3 260 002 kangaroos were killed under commercial harvest quotas, including 1 435 587 red kangaroos and 1 306 747 eastern greys. Kangaroo meat is sold either fresh, which is preferred, or frozen, to the pet food market. It has also become increasingly used as human food.

Koalas

At the time of European arrival, koalas ranged from SA to Qld. Their diet is mainly restricted to the leaves of specific varieties of eucalyptus trees. At one stage in the post-European arrival they were extensively hunted for their skins and in 1889, 300 000 skins were exported to London. By the 1930s koalas were extinct in SA, apart from Kangaroo Island. Total protection of koalas was proclaimed in Vic. in 1898, NSW in 1903 and SA in 1912. There was an open season on koalas in Qld in 1927 and 584 738 skins were taken. Koalas are now totally protected. In 1987–89, the National Koala Survey reported sightings of koalas in 696 localities.

On Kangaroo Island sustained browsing of preferred food species and the impact of this on tree health and longevity has emerged as the most important management issue on the island. The control of koala numbers on the island has become a major issue. Attention is being given to the translocation of some mainland species and methods of reducing the fertility of the population.

Possums

A predominantly arboreal marsupial, the possum varies widely in size and in ecological adaptation, from small mouse-like insect-eaters to large web-footed phalangers. There are gliders (feather-tailed glider, sugar glider, squirrel glider and greater glider), ringtails and brushtails. Some species are abundant, while others are rare or extinct, or thought to be extinct.

◗ Brushtail possums were hunted commercially for many years, their skins being sold overseas as opossum, skunk, beaver and chinchilla. They are now protected unless it can be shown that they are causing local damage.

◗ Leadbeater's possum, presumed extinct for over 50 years, was found again in 1961 at Marysville (Vic.).

Placental mammals
Bats

In Australia there are eight species of fruit or nectar-eating bats; the other 50 or so species all eat insects. The majority of species live in tree hollows, under bark or in rooftops. Apart from the large fruit bats (the flying foxes), most Australian bats are tiny, the largest weighing about 30 g and the smallest 2 or 3 g. Bats are vital participants in some ecosystems, having the important functions of regulating insect populations, pollinating flowers and spreading the seeds of many plant species.

Monotremes

Monotremes are warm-blooded animals that lay eggs and suckle their young and carry them in a pouch. There only two species worldwide: the platypus (native to Australia) and the echidna (native to both Australia and Papua New Guinea).

Platypus

The platypus is found from the north-eastern coastal region to the south-east of the continent and Tas. An aquatic animal, the platypus needs a good supply of bottom-dwelling aquatic life. While its environment has been considerably modified since the European arrival, the platypus is not presently in danger of extinction. However, its future may be threatened if the quality of waterways is adversely affected.

Echidna

The Australian short-beaked echidna (or spiny anteater) has a covering of fur and long spines, and is distributed throughout the continent. Its principal habitat requirement is a supply of the ants and termites upon which it feeds. The adult has no significant predator and the species is in no apparent danger.

Amphibians
Frogs

Frogs are the only Australian amphibians. There are 202 known species, of which 111 have been discovered since 1960. The largest species, the white-lipped tree frog, has a total length of 140 mm. The smallest species, the javelin tree frog, is as little as 14 mm in length. Land clearance, deforestation and salination of waterholes has caused a reduction in frog populations. In the last 15 years there have been serious declines of frog numbers and even possible extinctions.

Birds
Emus

The emu, a large, flightless, protected indigenous bird, has been farmed commercially. The first emu farm was established at Kalannie (WA) in 1970 to produce leather, but was abandoned in 1973. In 1981 the local Aboriginal community took over an emu farm which had been set up at Wiluna (WA) in 1976. There are many popular emu products, including leather, meat, oil, eggs (plain and carved), feathers and polished claws.

Short-tailed shearwaters (muttonbirds)

Muttonbirds nest in summer in burrows on islands in Bass Strait and on mainland Vic. and Tas., as well as in New Zealand. They are migratory birds that winter in the northern Pacific Ocean. A long-term banding program has provided information about the birds' habits. In 1992 a female, numbered 20 418, died. Over 38 years she had outlived two mates, produced 23 young and had covered about 1 million km on her migratory flights.

The shearwater was not hunted systematically before European arrival. The first harvest was in 1831, when about 112 000 birds were killed. They are now hunted during an annual open season from 23 March to 30 April, with their exploitation being mainly confined to the Furneaux group of islands. They are taken for human consumption, for their feathers (used for filling pillows) and for their oil (used in liniments).

Rare and endangered birds

The emus of Kangaroo Island, King Island (Tas.) and Tas. are the only birds acknowledged to have disappeared since the arrival of Europeans. There are hopes that three supposedly lost mainland species – the night parrot, the paradise parrot and the western rufous bristlebird – may be rediscovered. Mainland species which are threatened include the Cape Barren goose, the white pygmy goose, the freckled duck and the Burdekin duck. The Norfolk Island boobook, a small owl, is said to be the rarest bird in the world. In 1986 a female boobook was trapped, probably the sole survivor of her kind. A New Zealand owl, the mopoke, is closely related to the boobook and two males were released on Norfolk Island in 1987. In May 1998 there were 16 descendants from the matings.

▶ Considerable concern is now expressed about the number of wandering albatross, with its wingspan of 3.25 m, being killed when taking the baited hooks trailed by longline tuna fishing boats.

▶ It is also thought that a decline in the number of penguins on the sub-Antarctic islands may be caused by warming of Southern Ocean waters, which will affect the availability of krill, the penguins' main food supply.

▶ In May 1998 it was reported that infectious bursal disease, one of the most resistant viruses known, had escaped into colonies of Antarctic penguins. As all the penguins with the antibodies were found near Mawson Base, humans are presumed to have been the vectors for transmission of the disease.

Reptiles
Snakes
About 170 species of Australian snakes belonging to six major families are found on the continent or in surrounding waters. The viper family is not represented in Australia. Most Australian snakes are not aggressive unless provoked.

▶ The taipan, Australia's largest venomous snake, is found from NT to Qld.

▶ The tiger snake has one of the most potent venoms known to humans and is found from south-eastern Qld to south-western WA.

▶ A little-known relative of the taipan, the fierce snake or western taipan grows to 2 m and has the most toxic venom of any Australian snake, making it one of the world's deadliest snakes.

▶ Between 1980 and 1993, 33 people died as a result of snakebites.

Crocodiles
There are two species indigenous to Australia: the estuarine (or saltwater) crocodile and the freshwater crocodile. The former is one of the world's largest

crocodiles, with males usually growing to 5 m (with some up to 7 m recorded). Crocodiles are now farmed commercially for their meat and skins. Crocodiles detected in waters frequented by humans are trapped and taken to crocodile farms.

Sharks

Of the 350 species of sharks encountered worldwide, about 85 are found in Australian waters, varying in size from half a metre (the luminous shark) to 15 m (the world's largest shark, the whale shark). Included in the 85 species are 15 species of wobbegongs and catsharks, 25 whaler sharks and 14 dogfish. Several species of sharks have been identified in fatal unprovoked attacks on people: the white pointer (great white shark), the tiger shark and several species of whaler shark. Five other species are considered potentially dangerous: the wobbegong, the hammerhead, the blue shark, the mako and the grey nurse shark. Recently, steps have been put in place in Australia to list the white pointer as an endangered species as it is a slow breeder and is easily killed on account of its large size.

- The first recorded Australian shark attack was in 1791 on an Aboriginal woman on the north coast of NSW. Between 1791 and 1993 there were 523 reported shark attacks, 183 of which were fatal. Up to 76 of the attacks could possibly be attributed to the white pointer.
- In 1998 the Commonwealth government declared a shark-safe haven throughout Australian territorial waters for the great white shark and the grey nurse shark.
- The chances of being killed by shark attacks ranks low in accidental causes of death in Australia.

Selected accidental causes of death, Australia 1980–90

	Average per year
motor vehicle accidents	2979.3
scuba diving accidents	8.0
bee stings	1.8
lightning strikes	1.7
shark attacks	**1.0**
crocodile attacks	0.7

Whales, dolphins and dugongs

Forty-three species of whales, dolphins and porpoises are found in Australian waters, and are totally protected.

Whales

Whale-watching has taken the place of the commercial exploitation of species such as the humpback and southern right whales. Between 4500 and 7000 humpbacks are present in northern Australian tropical waters during the breeding season. In 1994 about 620 400 passengers/observers took part in whale-watching, with an estimated direct value of $8.8m. During 1995 there were 126 reported strandings of 18 species of whales and nine species of dolphins. Of these, 44 animals were found alive and 29 were released back into the sea.

Dolphins

About 35 species of dolphins, porpoises and other small cetaceans have been found in Australian waters, none of which are thought to be in danger of extinction.

Dugongs

Dugongs (sometimes called sea cows) belong to the order *Sirena* and are related to the manatee. The World Conservation Union has listed the dugong as 'vulnerable to extinction'. It is found in northern waters and is endangered by the limited period in which it can reproduce. The female has a long gestation period and only gives birth every 3–7 years. Dugong numbers are being reduced by accidental entanglement in shark nets, boat strikes and illegal catches.

Export and import of wildlife

There are strict controls over the export and import of wildlife. The Australian Customs Service detected 303 illegal imports or exports of wildlife in 1993–94, 408 in 1994–95 and 625 in 1995–96. Much of this increase is accounted for by the lucrative overseas market for Australian species, especially for birds, particularly certain species of parrots.

Feral animals

Some species of introduced feral animals have devastated Australian ecosystems. Feral herbivores eat out the vegetation which is the food supply and shelter for many native species. The impact of cloven hoofs and the rooting and wallowing of feral animals cause land degradation and affect agricultural production by damaging crops or by competing with domestic animals for grazing land and water supplies.

Rabbits

The feral rabbit is of European origin, arriving with the First Fleet in 1788. The initial spread of the animal was encouraged by deliberate releases into the wild or by accidental escapes. Rabbits degrade rural properties by their burrowing habits, their competition with stock on grazing lands and the additional degradation they cause by selective cropping of grass species. A single female rabbit is capable of producing up to 25 young in one year.

By 1890, efforts were being made to restrict the spread of the pest by erecting extensive rabbit-proof fences, such as the No. 1 Rabbit-Proof Fence in WA. This fence was completed in 1907 and extended 2059 km from Esperance in the south to Port Hedland in the north. The fences were ineffective as they were erected too late and were difficult to maintain. Other rabbit control methods have included ripping up burrows, poisoning, trapping and dogging, all of which are of limited effectiveness. In 1936 myxomatosis, a viral disease endemic to South America, was released, but it was not until 1950–51 that it had a devastating effect on the rabbit population, with numbers being dramatically reduced. However, in recent years rabbit numbers have increased as the virus became less virulent and rabbit immune systems became more resistant to it. In October 1995 the deadly rabbit calicivirus disease escaped to the mainland from an experimental trial on Wardung Island (SA). The Commonwealth government announced in September 1996 that subject to state and territory approval 20 infected rabbits would be released at about 200 sites. In August 1997 evidence emerged that the calicivirus disease was having mixed effects on the rabbit population, being more effective in drier regions.

Cane toads

The cane toad was imported from Hawaii in 1935 to act as a biological control of the cane beetles infesting the sugar cane fields. They had little effect on the beetle and have now spread throughout Qld, into northern NSW and into the Gulf of Carpentaria and eastern NT. They are indiscriminate feeders, eating indigenous snakes and lizards. They have poison cells in their skins and have caused the deaths of snakes, goannas, kookaburras, crows, bitterns, western native cats and dogs. At present there appears to be no effective method of controlling the toads.

⬩ The cane toad can live for up to 15 years and the females lay up to 30 000 eggs per year, compared with native frog species which mostly lay about 1000 eggs per year.

Feral pigs

The distribution of feral pigs is determined by a readily available, permanent water supply. They can increase at 80–110% per season depending on climatic conditions. As well as affecting natural ecosystems, they also eat and damage crops and pasture, damage fences and can kill and eat newborn lambs.

⬩ Some wild pigs are shot for their meat; in 1990, 1500 t of wild pig meat was exported to Europe.

Foxes

Commercial harvesting of foxes for fur was once a viable industry and served as a method of control. Furs have become largely unfashionable and the market value of fox skins is unstable. Foxes are now mainly controlled by shooting, trapping and poisoning.

Other feral pests

The Asian buffalo, cats, cattle, dogs, donkeys, goats, horses, rats and mice are other feral introduced animals which have impacted over a wide spectrum of the environment and economy.

Companion animals

In 1989 it was estimated that there were 788 000 owned dogs (excluding working dogs) and 849 000 owned cats in Vic. Only 457 127 dogs were registered with local authorities. In 1991 the cat population of SA was about 332 000, with 35.4% of households owning cats. It was estimated that unowned (stray) cats made up about 10% of the total cat population. Unfortunately, many domestic pets stray or are abandoned, becoming feral and threatening native animals or birds. Some lost and stray cats and dogs are received by animal shelters.

Royal Society for the Protection of Cruelty to Animals (RSPCA)

The RSPCA is the peak non-government organisation committed to the protection and care of animals. There are many smaller organisations which have similar objectives. The RSPCA has the power to prosecute people who are cruel to animals.

- In 1996–97 the RSPCA received over 158 000 animals from across Australia, including 69 956 dogs and 62 163 cats. As well, it took in 25 900 other animals, including horses, livestock, birds, native animals, ferrets, guinea pigs, penguins and a fur seal.
- Only 1.8% of the cats and 15.3% of the dogs received by the RSPCA are reclaimed by their owners. In 1996–97, the RSPCA found new homes for 25 479 dogs and 14 384 cats. They had to euthanise 46 663 cats and 33 794 dogs.

Household cats as predators

A survey in 1991 suggested that 50–60% of owned cats killed birds and small mammals and about 30% killed reptiles, and that in a year each cat took an average of eight birds, 16 mammals and eight reptiles. Legislation has been introduced in Vic. and SA requiring the registration of cats and giving local authorities the power to prosecute owners and impound and destroy stray animals.

Dog attacks on humans

In 1991–92 throughout Australia (except NT), there were 1313 cases in which dog attacks resulted in the hospitalisation of the victim. Of these, 557 cases involved children aged up to nine years. A 1991 Adelaide study showed that five specific breeds (German shepherds, bull terriers, pit bull terriers, dobermanns and rottweilers), which made up only 21.5% of the dog population, were involved in almost 75% of all dog attacks.

Insect pests
Blowflies
There are about 200 species of blowflies in Australia. Many are specialised parasites which perform a useful function as their larvae (maggots) feed upon carrion. The sheep blowfly causes severe economic losses in the sheep industry. Eggs are laid in soiled or moist areas of the fleece, particularly in the breech area. The maggots eat the region where they were laid, spoil the fleeces and often kill the sheep. Blowfly strike is an expense to the industry, which undertakes control measures such as docking the lambs' tails, removing wool or folds of skin from the breech area (crutching or mulesing), or the use of chemical compounds. The annual cost to the industry is estimated to be in excess of $150m.

Plague locusts
Serious damage can occur to pastures and crops when major outbreaks of the Australian plague locust occur, mainly in south-western Qld, NSW, SA and the NT. The adult locusts form dense swarms that can infest more than 20 km^2 and can migrate up to 500–600 km at night. Outbreaks can occur about every two years and there have been six major outbreaks in the last 50 years. It has been estimated that damage from the 1984 attack cost $358m. Control is most effective when the nymph locusts are sprayed with the insecticide fenitrothion.

Termites
Termites are primitive insects which have a social organisation

similar to ants, some bees and some wasps. Individual termites belong to several castes, all of which carry out specific tasks. Within a colony the queen termite may lay more than 1000 eggs each day, and may live for up to 20 years. The damage caused to houses and other buildings and to growing trees costs the economy millions of dollars each year. However, termites perform a useful function by devouring fallen branches and dead trees and ultimately returning organic material and its mineral content to the soil.

Spiders

There are many species of spider found in Australia, some of which are venomous, e.g. the red-back spider and the Sydney funnel web spider. The male funnel web is Australia's most deadly spider and its bite can cause death in as little as five minutes. In the period 1980–93 five people died from spider bites.

REGISTER OF THE NATIONAL ESTATE

The inventory of significant natural, historic and Aboriginal places is administered by the Australian Heritage Commission, which also nominates sites for World Heritage Listing and for the protection of Aboriginal heritage. In 1995–96 there were 836 Aboriginal sites of significance, 76 870 historic sites and 1791 natural sites on the register.

▶ In 1997–98 the Commonwealth government provided $10.1m for the identification and conservation of the National Estate.

▶ As a large proportion of Australia's heritage sites are in private ownership, the cost of conservation continues to be a major obstacle to heritage conservation. The Tax Incentive for

Heritage Conservation Scheme offers a 20% tax rebate for works which conserve, restore or adapt heritage buildings listed in the Register of the National Estate, with a cost to Commonwealth revenue of $1.9m.

▶ In 1996–97, 24 places were notified as being lost to the National Estate, three were destroyed by fire, 16 were demolished and three were relocated.

Nature conservation reserves

On 26 April 1879 the NSW government established the world's second national park, the Royal National Park (7300 ha) at Port Hacking (Sydney). In 1991 there were 3225 land nature reserves of various forms covering 41 million ha, and 228 marine and estuarine protected zones extending over 39 million ha – including 546 national parks, 616 other reserves and 273 natural places for the protection of endangered species. The national parks (mostly under state or territory control) and nature reserves make up about 5.5% of the continent.

Nature reserves have been established to protect unique ecosystems; most are isolated and not available for recreational purposes. There are nature reserves on several external territories and in Commonwealth waters: Norfolk Island (460 ha), Christmas Island (2370 ha), Ashmore Reef (58 300 ha), Elizabeth and Middleton reefs (188 000 ha), Coringa-Herald Reef and Lifou Reef. There is a 100 ha reserve on North Keeling Island, in the Cocos (Keeling) Islands, protecting the wreck of the German cruiser *Emden*, destroyed by HMAS *Sydney* on 4 November 1914.

World Heritage Listings

Thirteen Australian areas are inscribed on the World Heritage List:
- Great Barrier Reef (Qld)
- Uluru (Ayers Rock–Mount Olga) National Park (NT)
- Shark Bay (WA)
- Lord Howe Island group (off NSW)
- Fraser Island (off Qld)
- central eastern coast rainforest reserves
- wet tropics of north-east Qld
- Willandra Lakes region (NSW)
- Kakadu National Park (Stages 1 and 2) (NT)
- Tasmanian wilderness heritage area
- Australian fossil mammal sites, Riversleigh (Qld), Naracoorte (SA)
- Macquarie Island (south-east of Tas.)
- Heard and McDonald Islands.

The Natural Heritage Trust of Australia was set up in 1997, with the objective of conserving, repairing and replenishing Australia's natural capital infrastructure. The trust will have an expenditure package totalling $1.249bn from 1996–97 to 2001–02.

National trusts

The first of these, the National Trust of Australia, was formed in 1945. There are now trusts in all states and territories, which aim to further the conservation of lands, buildings, works and artefacts of heritage importance because of their educational, aesthetic, historic, architectural, artistic, scientific, natural history or cultural significance. Nationwide, there were 80 000 trust members in 1997.
- The National Trust is responsible for 283 properties; not all are owned by the trust, some are vested in its control, others are managed as a result of peppercorn rentals and suchlike. The trust has more than 23 000 listings of

buildings, urban areas, landscapes and individual sites not looked after by individual trusts.

LAND UTILISATION

In 1995–96, 346.3 million ha of land were used for agricultural purposes, representing 60.3% of the total land area. In 1993–94, 18 million ha were used for crops, 30.9 million ha were sown in pastures and grasses, and the balance was used for grazing or was lying idle or fallow.

Irrigation
In 1994, 2.4 million ha of crops and pastures were irrigated compared with 1.8 million ha in 1987. Of the total area under crops, 11.4% was irrigated in 1992–93.

Soil deficiency and fertilisers
Most Australian soils are deficient in phosphate and there are also significant deficiencies in sulphur, nitrogen and potassium. Single-strength superphosphate is the predominant fertiliser in use, more than half of it being used on pastures having moderate to good precipitation. In 1992–93, 2.76 million t of fertiliser were spread on 19.7 million ha.

THE ENVIRONMENT

In June 1994, 68.9% of Australians said they were concerned about environmental problems. The areas of most concern were air pollution, ocean pollution, destruction of trees/ecosystems, freshwater pollution and the depletion of the ozone layer.

Water supplies and sewage disposal
Australia has a comparatively high level of available water resources per capita, but it is largely a dry continent with most of its land being semi-arid or arid.

- There is a median rainfall of less

than 600 mm per annum in 80% of the country, and 50% has less than 300 mm.

▶ In 1994, 63.5% of Australians were satisfied with mains water, while 14.5% used filters for drinking. Households depending on rainwater tanks numbered 976 400, and 14.4% of Australians said their water supply was insufficient.

Sydney

The Tank Stream, which ran through Sydney when it was founded in 1789, was the settlement's water supply. Inevitably it became inadequate to meet the demand for water and it also became polluted. Streams around Sydney Cove were used for drainage and sewage disposal. Today, most of Sydney's sewerage is discharged through diffusers at the end of tunnels which extend several km into the ocean. In the outer western suburbs treated sewerage is discharged into rivers which become heavily polluted and subject to outbreaks of blue-green algae. Sydney now draws its water supplies from a system of reservoirs held behind dams, the principal reservoir being the Warragamba. In periods of low rainfall, restrictions are placed on the use of water.

Melbourne

For 22 years after its foundation, Melbourne took its water directly from the Yarra River. By the 1850s population growth and industrial expansion led to the construction of the city's first reservoir at Yan Yean. Melbourne has a system with sanitary sewers separated from stormwater drains. There is a 10 800 ha treatment farm at Werribee and after purification the final discharge into Port Phillip Bay is clear effluent.

Brisbane

The Brisbane–Ipswich area draws its water supply from the Brisbane

River and its tributaries. The main sewage system, serving about 400 000 people, utilises outfalls in the lower Brisbane River and its tributaries.

Adelaide

A low annual rainfall and a high evaporation rate has resulted in Adelaide and its surrounding rural areas having chronic water supply problems. Water drawn from the Murray River is an essential factor in SA's environment, with its pipelines servicing Adelaide and country towns extending as far as 300 km to the north. The city's sewerage is treated with the activated sludge method, using biological filters and stabilisation lagoons with separate sludge digestion.

Perth

Perth's principal water source is a series of reservoirs, with supplementation from the Mundaring Weir. Summer peak demand is met by the use of a system of artesian bores. The main sewage systems discharge treated effluent into the Indian Ocean. Smaller sewage plants discharge treated effluent into nearby sandy soils.

Pollution of the air
The ozone hole

Australia is affected by the depletion of the atmospheric ozone layer (the ozone hole) over the Antarctic. Permanent climatic changes as a result of the depletion of the ozone could cause many more health problems. Ultraviolet radiation (UVR) will have a direct influence on an increased occurrence of skin cancers, Australia already having the highest incidence in the world of malignant skin cancer. A 1% increase in UVR would increase the incidence of senile cataracts by an additional eight cases per 10 000 people each year.

▶ The depletion of the ozone is attributed to the release into the atmosphere of chlorofluorocarbons (CFCs). Since 1990 no one in Australia has been allowed to manufacture or import aerosol spray cans containing CFCs, and the use of CFCs to manufacture foam plastics is also being reduced.

Leaded petrol

Sales of leaded petrol in Australia declined from 14 712 ML in 1980 to 11 930 ML in 1990 and 7482 ML in 1995, largely reflecting increases in the proportion of vehicles using unleaded petrol.

Pollution of the waterways

Land-use changes have radically altered the water quality in many rivers, lakes, dams and reservoirs. These changes include the controlled water flow from dams and weirs, fertiliser run-off, flows from sewage outlets and contamination from detergents. Many waterways now contain drinking water unsuitable for humans or stock to drink or even for humans to use for recreational purposes. Outbreaks of toxic blue-green algae blooms are now common.

▶ In 1878 there was a large bloom on Lake Alexandrina (SA).

▶ An algal bloom in February 1993 killed hundreds of crabs in Adelaide's outer harbour.

▶ Blue-green algae blooms were of plague proportions in 1991–92 on large stretches of the Murray–Darling system and on the Hawkesbury River (NSW).

Waste management
Household waste

It has been estimated that private households generate about 50% of the total solid waste in Australia. Figures for 1989 showed that for the year households were responsible for 370 kg per person of waste collected by councils and contributed 48% to the total waste disposed of by councils.

▶ In the City of Mitcham, Adelaide, in 1995, 4.9 kg of hazardous waste per year was found in kerbside collections, of which 69.38% was paint, 20.4% dry-cell and car batteries and 2.9% pharmaceuticals.

Recycling

In 1993, 248 local government areas had kerbside recycling schemes available for 8.66 million people, or 49.1% of the population.

Proportion of households recycling selected materials

material recycled	% 1992	1996
paper	54.7	74.5
glass	55.3	73.4
old clothing/rags	63.3	66.6
cans	44.1	62.1
garden waste	47.3	50.8
kitchen/food waste	35.6	44.9
no recycling	15.3	9.4

Landfill disposal of waste

Landfill areas in the major cities have limited capacities and expected future usage. Many councils no longer have landfill sites within their own boundaries, and are required to transport waste to landfill sites in other areas or make use of transit stations.

▶ It was estimated in 1989 that Sydney had landfills occupying 850 ha, with an expected remaining capacity of 10 years.

Beverage containers

Lightweighting of beverage and other containers has been a major achievement in waste minimisation in the packaging industry. Between 1970 and 1990 the weight of aluminium cans was reduced by 32%, the average glass bottle by 50%, steel cans by 18% and PET (polyethylene terephthalate) bottles by 36%.

Waste paper

In 1994–95, 45 393 t of paper and

paperboard unsorted waste and scrap were exported, earning $7.81m.

Scheduled wastes

Scheduled wastes are by-products of industrial processes for which there are no environmentally safe methods of disposal, and hazardous wastes containing substances which remain dangerous to humans and other living organisms if released into the environment. At least 10 000 t per year of scheduled wastes need to be destroyed.

Environmental protection costs

A partial estimate of Australia's environmental protection costs for 1991–92 put the public sector's contribution at $2852.7m and the private sector at $2300m.

Clean Up Australia Day

On 8 January 1989, former solo round-the-world yachtsman Ian Kiernan organised a 'Clean Up the Harbour Day' in Sydney. There is now a national 'Clean Up Australia Day'. On the Clean Up Australia Day in 1996, 500 000 people collected 10 000 t of rubbish from 7000 sites in 800 cities and towns. The efficacy of the day is indicated by the fact that 20 000 t were removed in 1994. The 1994 Clean Up Day revealed the following statistics.

▶ Plastic comprised 42% of the total waste collected, 33% being general plastic and 9% polystyrene.

▶ It is estimated that every hour Australians dump 230 000 plastic bags and 50 t of plastic.

▶ Recyclable items collected included paper and cardboard (20% of the rubbish collected) and metal and aluminium (14%).

AN OVERVIEW

Population

There were 3.8 million people living in Australia (excluding the indigenous population) at the beginning of the 19th century. Until 1971 Aboriginal and Torres Strait Islander people were not included in the Australian census of population. The passing of a referendum proposal in 1967 ensured that they were included in censuses and that the Commonwealth government could make special laws for them. Previously the state governments had the powers to make laws for the indigenous population.

At the census conducted on 6 August 1991, the resident population of Australia was

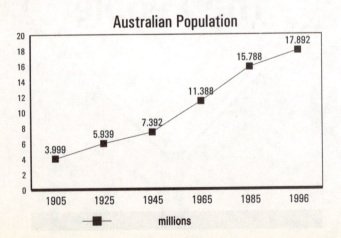

Australian Population

16 852 258, 8% above the 1986 census night, and on census night 1996 the population was 17 892 423 people, a growth of 1 040 165, or 6.2%, from the 1991 census.

- 94.6% persons counted were at home.
- There were 130 504 overseas visitors in Australia on census night 1996.
- In 1995 NSW was the most populous state (33.87%), followed by Vic. (24.94%) and Qld (18.15%).
- One projection of population growth suggests the population will reach about 25 million by the year 2045, with Qld being the state with the second highest population (5.7 million) by the year 2035.
- After making necessary statistical adjustments, the Australian Bureau of Statistics estimated that on 30 September 1997 the population was 18 588 600, and that the growth rate was 1.2% for the 12 months, compared with 1.3% for the year to 30 September 1996.

Population growth rates – states and territories

Year ended 30 September 1997	%
NSW	1.2
Vic.	1.2
Qld	1.8
SA	0.5
WA	1.8
Tas.	−0.4
NT	2.5
ACT	0.1

Projected growth rate, 2000–20

	%
Australia	**1.0**
Canada	0.9
France	0.2
Greece	−0.2
Japan	−0.4
New Zealand	0.6
Sweden	0.3
United Kingdom	0.2
United States	0.8

Population density, 1995 (average no. per km²)

Australia	2
Canada	3
France	105
Germany	228
Japan	331
New Zealand	13
Sweden	20
United Kingdom	238
United States	28

Males and females in the population

There were 8 849 224 males (49.5%) males and 9 043 199 females (50.5%) in the Australian population at the time of the 1996 census.

Age distribution of population

An overall ageing of the population has resulted from Australians having smaller families, with a resultant lower proportion of children. This trend has been accompanied by a marked increase in life expectancy.

▶ About 25% of the population was under 15 years in 1911; by 1995 this had fallen to 18% and it is estimated to fall further to about 14% by 2051.

▶ In 1971 the median age of the Australian population was 27.5 years, in 1991 it was 32.5 years and in 1996 34 years. It is predicted to be 42.6 years by 2051 and that 23.1% of the population will then be aged 65 years or more.

▶ 12.1% of the population were aged 65 years and over in 1996.

▶ In 1995 the median age of Australians was 34 years. In Indonesia 33% of the population were aged 0–14 years, with only 4% aged 60 years and over. For Papua New Guinea (PNG) the same proportions were 40% and 5%.

Median age, 1996

	years
NSW	34
Vic.	33
Qld	33
SA	35
WA	33
Tas.	34
NT	29
ACT	30
Australia	34

Population growth rate

The national growth rate was 1.2% in 1996–97, compared with 1.3% in the previous year. The decrease was mainly due to a reduced net overseas migrant intake.

◗ The net gain from overseas migration was 95 800, 8% fewer than 1995–96.

◗ There was an increase in permanent and long-term departures, from 153 100 in 1995–96 to 166 600 in 1996–97.

Life expectancy

The life expectancy of the Australian population has been governed to a large extent by higher standards of living, improved nutrition and the decreased incidence of many diseases. A marked decline in infant mortality also bears upon life-expectancy rates, as does deaths of young men from motor traffic accidents and the incidence of heart disease in older men. In the period 1881–90, the life expectancy at birth in Australia was 47.19 years for males and 50.84 for females. By 1946–48 it was 66.07 for males and 70.63 for females.

◗ In common with many other countries Australian women can expect to live longer than men. In 1994 Australian females had a life expectancy of 80.9 years and males 74.5 years.

◗ For children born in the period 1994–96 life expectancy in Australia was 75.2 years for males and 81.1 years for females.

Life expectancy, in years – at birth

	males	females
Australia (1994)	**74.5**	**80.9**
Canada (1992)	74.9	81.4
France (1992)	73.8	82.3
Germany (1993)	75.0	80.4
Japan (1993)	76.5	83.1
New Zealand (1992)	74.2	79.2
Sweden (1992)	75.5	81.1
United Kingdom	73.7	79.2
United States	72.2	79.2

Geographical distribution of the population

There is a sustained tendency for the population to be concentrated in the capital and other major cities on the southern and eastern coasts. On 30 June 1996 77% of the population was living in the three eastern states. However, in recent years there has been a significant growth in the population of Perth and adjacent parts of WA.

Urban population, 1995

	%
Australia	**85**
Canada	77
France	73
Germany	87
Japan	78
New Zealand	86
Sweden	83
United Kingdom	89
United States	76

▶ For both the Australian-born and overseas-born sections of the population there has been a significant decline in the proportion living in rural areas. In 1921 62.1% of the population lived in urban areas, in 1991 85.3% did so.

Regional population growth

Between 1991 and 1996 the Local Government Areas (LGAs) with the largest percentage population increases were Caboolture Shire (Qld) at 7.3%, Rockingham City (WA) at 6.9%, Maroochy Shire (Qld) at 5.7% and Swan Shire (WA) at 5.5%. The largest declines were in East Pilbara Shire (WA) at −7.2%, Roebourne Shire (WA) at −2.8%, Elizabeth City (SA) at −2.4 % and the Moree Plains Area (NSW) at −1.7%.

▶ Among the Statistical Location Areas (SLAs) Broken Hill, in the far west of NSW, had a population loss of 2400, a decline of 10%, with losses in all age groups.

▶ The SLA with the largest growth was Liverpool City, in the western environs of metropolitan Sydney, where the population grew by 23 100 or 23%.

Population turnover

The NT at 23% and the ACT at 17% had the highest rates of population turnover in 1996–97.

Migration

Population growth has often been a response to economic conditions, e.g. the Great Depression, or particular social events, e.g. the two World Wars. Australia's Baby Boom years were 1946–60, with a natural increase rate of 1.46%. It was government policy that Australia's population should reach an annual growth rate of 2%, and an immigration program began aimed at increasing the population by 1% per annum. The average growth rate for this period was 2.26%.

Components of population growth

Population growth is determined by two factors: (a) natural increase, i.e. the difference between births and deaths, and (b) net overseas migration, i.e. the difference between permanent arrivals and permanent departures.

◗ The fastest population growth since 1901 took place from 1946 to 1960, with an average annual growth rate of 2.26%. The second highest was 1901–13 at 2.04%.

◗ The proportional contributions of natural increase and net migration to population growth have changed significantly since 1982–83. Net migration at times has exceeded natural increase, e.g. in 1989–90.

Immigration

In the 1850s, mainly as a result of racial pressures on the goldfields, restrictions were imposed on the entry of Chinese, a policy later applied to other non-Caucasians and incorporated into the White Australia policy which remained in force until the 1970s. Throughout the 20th century immigration has been largely directed by government policy and responses in other countries and within Australia. Permanent and long-term movements are the elements of net overseas migration which affect the resident population.

- A planned migration program was commenced in 1945, and as a result 5 million people have made their homes in Australia.

During 1991–95 320 000 net permanent migrants were added to the Australian population. Permanent arrivals are now accepted in the categories of family reunion, skilled, humanitarian (including refugee) and from New Zealand. In 1995–96 there were 99 140 permanent arrivals, compared to the peak figure of 145 300 in 1988–89. The continued high rate of unemployment in Australia was the reason given for a drastic reduction in the immigration intake. The 1997–98 program maintains refugee and humanitarian places at 12 000, but the non-humanitarian program has been cut to 68 000 from 74 000. The family reunion section of the program is reduced to 32 000, with the parent reunion numbers decreasing from 6000 to 1000.

- There were 263 100 permanent and long-term arrivals in the 12 months to September 1996 and 261 767 in the 12 months to 30 September 1997.
- In 1995–96 there were 99 100 settler arrivals, 13% more than 1994–95, the largest group being New Zealand-born (12 300 or 12.4%). UK-born (11 300 or 11.4%) made up the second largest group and Chinese-born (11 200 or 11.3%) the third highest.
- The median age of the overseas-born population in 1996 is 44 years compared with the Australian-born 34 years; it is influenced by the time of peak periods of arrival in Australia by the various ethnic communities, e.g. the Korean-born population in Australia has an average age of 29 years, those from PNG 28 years,

Singapore 27 years, the former USSR and the Baltic States 65 years, Hungary 58 years, Greece 55 years and Poland 54 years.

▶ As at 30 June 1995, 23% of the Australian population was born overseas.

▶ Since 1900 4.5 million people have been added to the population as a result of net overseas migration.

▶ 44% of the permanent and long-term arrivals in 1994–95 intended to settle in NSW.

Age and sex of migrants

Permanent arrivals are generally younger than the population as a whole. In 1994–95 the mean age of the new settlers was 28 years compared with 33.7 years for the population as a whole.

▶ There were 87 males for every 100 females arriving in 1994–95, but the sex ratio tends to fluctuate to a marked degree from one year to the next.

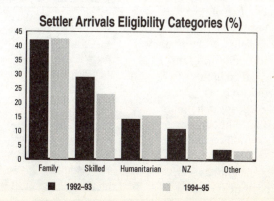

Boat people

During 1996–97 365 people arrived in Australia by boat without authorisation, a decrease of more than 40% on 1995–96. By 26 June 1997 a total of 2779 boat people had arrived since 1989, of whom 763 were children.

◗ Seventy-five children have been born while their mothers have been in detention.

◗ Five hundred and twenty-five boat people have been granted entry and 359 remain in Australia.

◗ The detention camp at Port Hedland, WA, holds 209 detainees.

◗ Ninety-two people, of whom many had been detained for up to three years, were deported in July 1997.

Coastal surveillance

In 1995–96 3228 Coastwatch flights flew a total of 14 215 hours over approximately 43 million nautical square miles.

◗ 74 000 separate sightings were reported to Coastwatch clients.

Overstayers

In 1994–95 8860 persons were located who had overstayed their visitor visa entry permits or who admitted to working illegally.

◗ As at 30 June 1996 there were 45 100 visa overstayers in Australia.

◗ Visitors from the United Kingdom are at the top of the total list of overstayers at 18%, however the high volume of tourism means that the actual percentage of British overstayers is very low.

Top ten overstayers, 1997

	% of legal visitors who overstay
Syria	3.1
Bangladesh	2.5
Western Samoa	2.5
Tonga	2.5
Colombia	2.4
Cambodia	1.6
Burma	1.4
Pakistan	1.2
Vietnam	1.2
Turkey	1.1
Lebanon	1.0

Main countries of birth of the Australian population

Apart from the Australian-born, in 1995 there were 1 210 900 people born in the United Kingdom and Ireland living in Australia, 290 100 born in New Zealand, 261 400 born in Italy, 179 800 born in Yugoslavia and 144 700 born in Greece. In the 1996 census 76.99% of people counted were born in Australia, 6.6% in the UK or Ireland, 1.62% in NZ, 1.41% in Italy, 1.01% in the former Yugoslav republic. No other country represented more than 1% of the Australian population.

▶ Among the states and territories, at the time of the 1996 census, Tas. had the highest proportion of people born in Australia, at 85.9%, whereas WA had the lowest at 68.3%.

▶ 76.4% of all overseas-born people were in NSW, Vic. and Qld.

▶ 52.8% were located in Sydney and Melbourne.

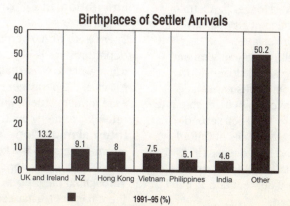

Birthplaces of Settler Arrivals

UK and Ireland	NZ	Hong Kong	Vietnam	Philippines	India	Other
13.2	9.1	8	7.5	5.1	4.6	50.2

1991–95 (%)

Citizenship

Before the passing of the *Nationality and Citizenship Act 1948*, which came into effect on Australia Day 1948, Australians were British subjects. Since that date up to the end of December 1995 there have been 2.8 million grants of citizenship to people born outside Australia, giving a citizenship rate of 60.3% of the total overseas-born population.

▶ 93.9% of the Greek-born population, who generally are older and have lived longer in Australia than other migrant groups, have taken out citizenship.

▶ 71.4% of those born in Vietnam have been granted citizenship.

▶ People from English-speaking countries have a low citizenship rate.

▶ There were 1 460 600 second-generation Australians of United Kingdom and Irish descent in 1991, 327 300 of Italian descent, 167 600 of New Zealand descent and 151 200 of Greek descent.

▶ On census night 1996, 15 888 961 persons were Australian citizens.

Grants of Australian citizenship, 1996–97

former countries of citizenship	
Britain (including Hong Kong)	27 294
New Zealand	19 982
China (PRC)	16 173
Vietnam	5083
Philippines	3815
former Yugoslavia	3207
India	2563

Emigration and permanent departures

There were 28 700 permanent departures in 1995–96, a third of whom went to New Zealand.

▶ 44% of the permanent departures were former settlers, with 75% returning to their country of birth.

Internal migration

Internal migration is a key element in the distribution of population. Throughout the present century there has been a marked shift of

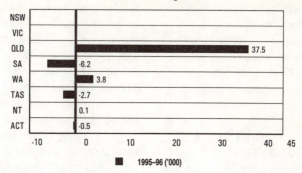

Inter-state Migration

	1995–96 ('000)
NSW	
VIC	
QLD	37.5
SA	-6.2
WA	3.8
TAS	-2.7
NT	0.1
ACT	-0.5

population from rural to urban areas. In 1911 43% of the population lived in rural areas. The rural population fell to 14% in 1976 and has since steadied at about 15%. In recent times there has been a marked interstate migration. People have tended to move from the southern states to Qld and to WA.

Net estimated internal migration, for year ended 30 June 1997

NSW	–13 610
Vic.	–6307
Qld	3431
SA	–5185
WA	5216
Tas.	–3713
NT	1800
ACT	–6682

Racial discrimination

Since 1991 the Commonwealth Human Rights and Equal Opportunity Commission has received a total of 2806 complaints relating to the *Racial Discrimination Act*.

▶ 23.2% concerned Aborigines and

Torres Strait Islanders, 41.8% people of a non–English speaking background and 16.7% people of an English speaking background, with the ethnicity of the complainant not stated in 18.3% of cases. A high proportion of cases are dismissed following a 'no case' submission.

Aborigines and Torres Strait Islanders

An Aborigine or Torres Strait Islander is a person of Aboriginal or Torres Island descent, who identifies as an Aborigine or Torres Strait Islander and who is accepted as an Aborigine or Torres Strait Islander by the community in which he or she lives. There is no accurate means of estimating the numbers of the indigenous population at the time of the European arrival, with various estimates ranging from 300 000 to 1 million. Aborigines numbered 206 104 in the 1991 census and there were 21 541 Torres Strait Islanders.

Aborigines represented 1.3% of the total population and Torres Strait Islanders 0.1%. The indigenous population is estimated to have grown at a rate of 3.4% in the period 1986–91. However, at the 1996 census 352 970 people identified themselves as being of indigenous origin, an increase of 33%. This high rate of increase cannot be due to natural causes and is in part explained by an increased willingness by people to declare their indigenous origin.

- In 1996, 314 120 of the indigenous population were Aborigines, 28 744 were Torres Strait Islanders and 10 100 were of both Aboriginal and Torres Strait Islander descent.
- 55.8% of indigenous people were in two states: NSW (101 485) and Qld (95 518). 14.4% (45 233) were in WA and 14.7% (46 277) in the NT. They represented 3% or less of the total population in each state and territory, except the NT, where they

were 23% of the total population.

The age structure of the Aboriginal and Torres Strait Islander population is very young compared with the rest of Australia: 38% of the indigenous population is aged under 15 and 4% over 60. High fertility rates among indigenous women are largely a cause of this age structure. In the 1960s indigenous women had an average of six children; that rate had decreased to about 3 in the 1980s, compared with a rate of 1.9 for all Australian women. High death rates also affect the age structure, as does a life expectancy of about 57 for males and 64 years for females.

Aboriginal and Torres Strait Islander Land Fund

The Land Fund and Indigenous Land Corporation (ATSIC Amendment) Act 1995 provides for the establishment of the Aboriginal and Torres Strait Islander Fund. From 1995–96 to 2003–04 $121m (indexed) will be appropriated to the Land Fund from the Commonwealth government each year, with about 66% invested to build up the capital base of the Fund.

▶ In 1996–97 the Indigenous Land Council approved the purchase of 44 properties and 15 purchases were settled.

BIRTHS

There were 253 955 live births registered in Australia in the year ended 30 June 1997, an increase of 0.6% over the 252 342 of the previous year.

▶ There were 105.9 boys per 100 girls born in 1996.

Crude birth rates

The crude birth rate is calculated from the number of live births per 1000 of population. In 1996 the Australian birth rate was 13.8 compared with 21.7 in 1971.

▶ In 1880–82 the crude birth rate was 30.

▶ SA, at 12.6, had the lowest

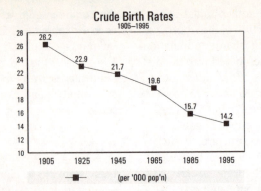

birth rate in 1996, compared with the highest rate of the NT at 19.1.

Ex-nuptial births

Ex-nuptial births represented 5.3% of all live births in 1914 and 9.3% in 1971. In 1996 69 568 or 27.4% of all births were ex-nuptial.

▶ Paternity for 84.1% of ex-nuptial births was acknowledged at the time of birth registration.

Fertility rates and family size

The fertility rate is the number of children that would be born per woman if she were to live to the end of her child-bearing age, and bear children in according to the prevailing age-fertility rates. The fertility rate is an indication of the

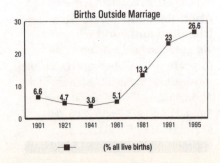

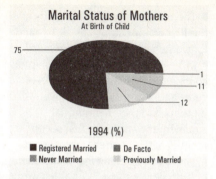

extent to which a population reproduces itself.

▶ In 1961, at the peak of the Baby Boom, the rate peaked at 3.6, falling away to 2.9 by 1966. The availability of the contraceptive pill, a desire for smaller families and the extended entry of women into the work force have been contributing factors in the decline of the fertility rate.

▶ The 1994 fertility rate for the general population in WA was 1.9, while for WA indigenous women it was 2.4.

▶ Australia's fertility rate fell just below 1.8 children per women of child-bearing age in 1996, for the first time since records were kept. There has been a steady decline in the rate since 1992.

Fertility of Aboriginal women

The average number of children born to Aboriginal and Torres Strait Islander women aged 20–24 years is three times that of non-Aboriginal women. For each older age group Aboriginal fertility is higher than for the general population.

Age-specific birth rates

The age-specific birth rate is calculated from the number of live births registered in a calendar year according to the age of the mother, per 1000 females of the same age, estimated at 30 June.

▶ There has been a trend towards women beginning child-bearing later in life and rearing smaller families.

▶ The average age in 1993 of all mothers was 28.2 years and 26.2 for those having their first baby.

Teen-age births
women aged 15–19 years per '000 of pop'n, 1994

Australia	21
Canada	27
France	9
Germany	13
Japan	4
New Zealand	35
Sweden	13
United Kingdom	33
United States	64

Confinements

A confinement is a pregnancy that results in at least one live birth.

- In 1996 3168 mothers aged 40 and over had confinements, of whom 319 had had five or more children during their current marriage.
- 5% of all confinements were with mothers under 20 years of age. 1.9% of all confinements were for mothers aged 40 years and over.
- There were 1776 first-nuptial confinements for women aged 40 and over.
- The median age of the parents at the first confinement was 29.2 years for women and 31.9 years for men.
- In 1994 there were 1104 first-nuptial confinements to marriages of 10–14 years and 338 of 15 years or over; 7660 mothers had their first-nuptial confinement within the first seven months of their current marriage.
- There has been an increased use of birth centres. 251 797 babies were born in hospitals in 1993 and 3400 in birth centres.

Caesarean births

In the late 1960s the incidence of caesarean births was 4% of all births. Today, almost one in five of all children born in Australia is delivered by caesarean section. In 1993, 48 778 (19%) of birth deliveries were by caesarean section; 23.6% of caesarean sections were performed on women with private health insurance and 16.45% on women with public health insurance. In Qld the rate of caesarean births was 58%

higher in private hospitals than in public hospitals.

Multiple births
Multiple births resulted from 1.4% of all confinements in 1996.

IVF and GIFT babies
Infertile couples are increasingly being assisted to achieve pregnancies as a result of treatment by either in vitro fertilisation (IVF) or gamete intrafallopian transfer (GIFT).

- Of the 2300 pregnancies conceived from IVF in 1994, 745 resulted in live births.
- 17% of IVF and 27% of GIFT pregnancies resulted in multiple births.

Contraception
In 1995, 45% of women aged 15–49 years reported that they or their partner currently used some form of contraception; 27.1% used the contraceptive pill and 12% used a condom.

- 2.1% used natural methods, e.g. rhythm/Billings etc.
- 1.7% relied on withdrawal, diaphragm and other methods.

Termination of pregnancy
Only SA and NT collect population-based data on induced abortions. In SA in 1994 there were 19 519 confinements and 5139 induced abortions (about one in five). Half of all SA teenage pregnancies were terminated.

Birth weight
Except in Vic., babies born to indigenous women are more likely than the babies of non-indigenous women to be of low birth weight (less than 2500 g).

- In 1995 11.8% of indigenous infants had a low birth weight, almost twice the national average.

Postnatal stays in hospital
The proportion of mothers staying less than four days in hospital was 35.5% in 1995, as compared with 20.2% in 1991.

- Mothers without health insurance were two and a half times more likely to stay postnatally in hospital for less than five days than insured mothers.

Breastfeeding

Length of period of breastfeeding, 1995

	%
never	12.4
less than one week	1.9
two weeks or more	77.7
two months or more	68.1
six months or more	47.1
one year or more	15.3

◗ 45% of boys and 68% of girls of single-parent families are more likely not to have been breastfed for at least three months.

◗ 90% of Aboriginal children in the NT now under 13 years of age were breastfed; in NSW, Vic. and SA more than 33.3% of Aboriginal children now under 13 years of age were not breastfed.

Birth defects

About 4300 (1.6%) children are born each year with significant birth defects, diagnosed at birth or soon afterwards.

◗ Mothers aged 40 years and over have a childbirth malformation rate twice that of mothers aged 20–24 years.

◗ Birth defects accounted for one in five perinatal deaths and one in three infant deaths in 1994.

Adoptions

In 1971–72, 9798 adoptions were recorded; in 1975–76, the number had fallen to 4990, and in 1979–80 to 3337.

◗ In 1995–96 only 668 adoptions were recorded in Australia.

◗ The Supporting Mothers' Benefit introduced in July 1973 meant that for young unmarried mothers parenting their children became a realistic option.

DEATHS

There were 129 085 deaths registered in Australia in the year ended 30 June 1997, 3884 more than the same period the previous year. The crude death rate is the number of deaths per 1000 of population. In 1901 the rate was 12.2; it fell to 8.7 in 1920 and 8.6 in 1961. The death rate is a reflection of a range of social factors, including improved health standards, better nutrition and the ageing of the population.

▶ In 1994 the male crude death rate was 8.7 and the female rate was 5.2.

▶ The 1996 crude death rate was 7. The male rate was 8.2 and the female rate was 5.

▶ The median age at death in 1996 was 74 years for males and 80.7 for females.

▶ Married people as a whole in 1996 had lower death rates than those who were divorced, widowed or never married.

▶ In 1996 males aged 20–69 years who had never married had death

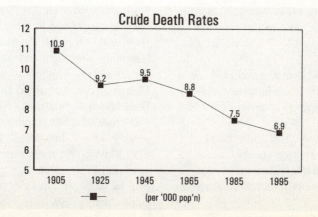

Crude Death Rates
(per '000 pop'n)

rates 2–4 times higher than those who had married.

Deaths from cancer

Australia has one of the world's highest rates of skin cancer (malignant melanomas). In 1996 585 males and 326 females died as a result of skin cancer. In 1995 about 80% of both men and women said that in the month prior to the survey, they had taken sun-protection measures. Deaths from melanomas of the skin have increased in males from 1083 in 1970–74 to 4259 in 1990–94; for females the corresponding figures were 786 and 1520.

▶ In 1996 5239 males and 2144 females died from lung cancer; 96% of these were people aged over 50 years.

▶ During 1996, 2660 men died of cancer of the prostate, 97% being cases aged over 60 years. In 1982 there were 1355 deaths from prostate cancer.

Prostate cancer, age-standardised death rate per 100 000 males, 1992

Australia	63.4
Canada	64.7
England and Wales	28.0
Italy	26.8
Japan	6.8
Netherlands	39.6
New Zealand (non-Maori)	37.8
United States (white)	100.8

About one in 200 female deaths in 1995 was caused by cervical cancer. It has been estimated that 90% of cervical cancer deaths are preventable through the use of biennial screening (pap smears) to detect early cell abnormalities.

Deaths from Acquired Immune Deficiency Syndrome (AIDS)

AIDS-related deaths increased steadily from 231 in 1988 to 738 in 1994. During 1995 there were 813 new cases of HIV infection diagnosed, the rate varying from 206.8 per 100 000 of population in NSW to 16.9 in Tas. Of

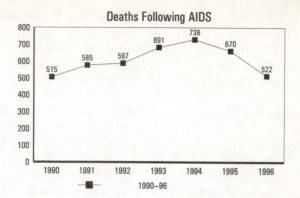

Deaths Following AIDS, 1990–96

the cases diagnosed 741 were males and 72 females.

- 42% of males who died were aged 30–39 years and an additional 31% were aged 40–49.

HIV cases diagnosed, 1995

Age	Males	Females
0–12	2	5
13–19	5	10
20–29	233	20
30–39	283	26
40–49	146	8
50–59	49	3
60+	23	–

By the end of 1996 it was estimated that there were 11 080 people in Australia with the HIV infection.

- Since 1987, of the 20 299 newly diagnosed HIV infection cases, 95% were males. The median age of infected males was 32 years, and 29 for infected females.
- NSW accounted for 63.5% of the newly diagnosed HIV infection cases.
- 96% of the total of AIDS-related deaths in 1996 were of males. Of these, 43% were aged 30–39 years, 29% 40–49 years and 14% 50–59 years.

Road accident deaths

There were 1765 road fatalities in the period July 1997–June 1998, compared with 1873 in the previous corresponding period, a fall of 5.7%. Of those killed 1228 (69.6%) were male and 537 (30.4%) were female.

Accidental falls

Falls caused the deaths of 523 males and 579 females in 1996, with 326 males and 525 females being 65 years and over.

Deaths from drowning and submersion

During 1994 208 males and 41 females drowned; many instances involved young children who died in backyard swimming pools, farm dams or similar situations. In 1993 30% of all drownings were of children aged 1–4 years and 7.6% aged 5–14 years. In 1994 25 children drowned in baths, 12 were infants and seven were aged one or two years.

Deaths from fire or scalding

There were 135 deaths in 1993 from fires, flames and scalds: 59% from house fires, 10% from clothing ignition and 10% from contact with a hot object, hot water or steam.

Deaths from childhood diseases

In 1920 482 children died from measles, 561 from whooping cough and 805 from diphtheria. By 1990 deaths from these diseases had no statistical significance.

Immunisation has much reduced the impact of childhood communicable diseases, but they have not been conquered. Between 1981 and 1995, when immunisation had been available for many years, 30 child deaths were caused by measles. The level of immunisation has fallen away, with recent data indicating that 91% of children are fully immunised.

Infant mortality

The infant mortality rate is the annual number of deaths of children

under one year of age per 1000 live births. In 1902 Australia had an infant mortality rate of 107.5. In 1993 the infant mortality rate was 6.1.
▶ Between 1986 and 1996 the infant mortality rate declined by 34%.
▶ In 1996 the indigenous infant mortality rates were 12.6 in SA, 24.1 in WA and 19.4 in the NT.

Infant mortality, per '000 live births

1901	103.8
1921	66.7
1941	39.7
1961	19.5
1981	10.0

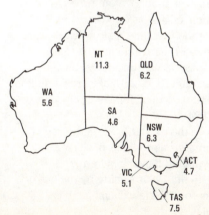

Infant Mortality
States and Territories, 1994
(per '000 Live Births)

Perinatal deaths

Perinatal deaths are those at or about birth, or when infants are born alive but die within 28 days of birth. The rate is calculated per 1000 live births. Perinatal deaths include foetal deaths (stillborns) and neonatals (those born alive but dying with 28 days). The Australian perinatal death rate was 13.2 in 1981; in 1996 it had fallen to 8.5. Of the 2170 deaths 65% were foetal deaths.
▶ The foetal death rate per 1000 births was 5.6 for males and 5.3 for females.

Maternal mortality

During the triennium 1988–90 there was an increase in maternal mortality resulting from obstetric complications to 12.7 per 100 000 confinements, compared to a rate of 11.8 in 1985–87. This has been attributed to more maternal deaths among Aboriginal women.

Maternal mortality, per 100 000 births, 1992

Australia	3.4
Canada (1991)	2.9
France (1991)	11.9
Germany	6.7
Japan	9.2
New Zealand (1991)	15.0
Sweden (1990)	3.2
United Kingdom	6.7
United States (1991)	7.9

Sudden Infant Death Syndrome (SIDS)

SIDS (also known as cot death) caused 397 infant deaths in 1979; the figure reached 531 in 1987 and declined to 507 in 1990. By 1995 SIDS had further declined to 220. There is considerable on-going research into the cause of SIDS. Parents have been encouraged to have their babies sleep on their backs, which is considered to be one of the factors in the decline in the number of deaths.

Pharmaceutical poisoning

In 1992–93 six females were hospitalised for every male as a result of poisoning from tranquillisers, sedatives, analgesics, opiates, anti-infectives and other pharmaceuticals.

Suicide

Each year almost four times as many men suicide as do women. In 1991 for the first time male suicides were greater than male deaths caused by motor-vehicle accidents. Suicide accounted for 2.9% of all male deaths and 0.9% of all female deaths in 1994.

▶ In the period 1979–93 the use of firearms as a means of suicide equalled hanging in frequency.

▶ In the 1990s suicide by the use of motor-vehicle exhaust gas has increased.

Deaths by murder

1993 saw 329 persons suffering homicide deaths, 35% by stabbing or cutting, 19% by shooting, 8% from unarmed fighting and 5% from child abuse and battering.

Organ donation

Since 1965 more than 25 000 Australians have received organ or tissue transplants, Australia having one of the world's highest transplant success rates. Australia has a low donor rate, about 10 donations per million of population. The Australian Co-ordinating Committee on Organ Registries and Donations (ACCORD) aims to raise the rate to between 14 and 15 donations per million of population.

▶ About 2500 Australians were on organ and corneal transplant waiting lists in January 1997.

▶ The organ and tissue donations from one person can benefit as many as nine people.

MARRIAGE

The marriage rate is the number of marriages per 1000 of population, and is subject to variation according to economic conditions and social attitudes. It was 7.32 in 1901, fell to 6 in 1931, peaked at 12 in 1942 and was 5.8 in 1996. The percentage of marriages with both parties not having married previously has remained stable. In 1995 the rate for marriages where both parties had never previously married was 68%, compared with 67% in 1985.

▶ On census night 1996, of the people in Australia aged 15 years and over 7.47 million were married, 471 074 were separated, and 898 834 were divorced. 171 326 males and 727 045 females were widowed. 2.35 million males and 1 941 876 females had never married.

Age at marriage

Among the factors affecting the mean age of marriages are the increase in the numbers of de facto marriages, women seeking employment opportunities and young people seeking extended educational opportunities.

First marriage

In 1996, for first marriages, 28.5% of grooms were aged 24 years and under, and 51.4% of brides were 24 years and under.

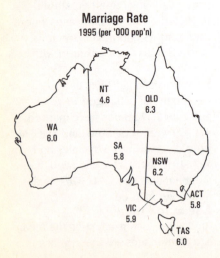

Marriage Rate
1995 (per '000 pop'n)

NT 4.6
QLD 6.3
WA 6.0
SA 5.8
NSW 6.2
ACT 5.8
VIC 5.9
TAS 6.0

Previous marital status

During 1996, 70 438 marriages were the first marriage for both parties, 19 657 marriages were the first marriage for one partner and 16 008 were remarriages for both parties.

Remarriages

The remarriage rate (per 1000 widowed and divorced males and females) has declined. In 1995 the peak age groups for remarriage were 30–34 years for men and 25–29 for women.

▶ The mean age of remarriage for men and women previously widowed was 62.5 years and 53.5 years respectively in 1995.

▶ For those previously divorced the mean age for remarriage in 1995 was 41.1 years for men and 37.6 years for women.

Category of marriage celebrants

In 1994 40.4% of marriages were performed by civil celebrants, compared with 33% in 1979. The NT had the highest proportion (62.1%)

of marriages performed by civil celebrants and Vic. the lowest (39%). 21% of marriages were performed in Roman Catholic churches in 1978, 17% in Anglican churches and 14% in Presbyterian or Uniting churches. By 1994 the percentages had fallen to 19.6%, 12.9% and 9% respectively.

◗ 53.2% of marriages were performed by ministers of religion in 1996.

De facto marriages

A considerable factor in the decline in the crude marriage rate has been the increase in the incidence of de facto marriages. In 1992 56% of couples had lived in a de facto relationship before marriage compared with 16% in 1975. 30% of couples had lived in a de facto relationship for five years or more and 11% had lived together for 10 years or more.

◗ In 1992 5% of all persons aged over 15 years were living in de facto relationships. De facto relationships are most common among the 25–29 age group (12%) and the 20–24 group (11%).

◗ Women in de facto relationships tended to be younger than those in registered marriages. About 70% of women in de facto relationships are under 36 years, compared with 29% of women in legalised marriages.

Marriage rate, per 1000 of population

Australia (1994)	6.2
Canada (1994)	5.4
France (1992)	4.7
Germany (1994)	5.4
Japan (1994)	6.3
New Zealand (1994)	6.3
Sweden (1992)	3.9
United Kingdom (1993)	5.9
United States (1993)	9.0

Divorce

The *Family Law Act 1975*, which established the Family Court of

Australia, provides that irretrievable breakdown is the only ground on which a divorce is granted. The breakdown of a marriage is confirmed by the husband and wife living apart for 12 months or more, with no reasonable possibility of reconciliation. The implementation of the law led to a marked surge in the divorce rate until 1979, since when the rate has steadied. In 1995 there were 12.3 divorces granted per 1000 married couples. The crude divorce rate in 1995 was 2.8 per 1000 of population.

▶ Approximately four out of 10 first marriages are terminated by divorce.
▶ In 1996, of all the applications for divorce lodged, 22% were joint applications, 46% were lodged by women and 32% by men.
▶ The duration of the marriage of parties divorcing in 1996 averaged 11 years, compared with 7.7 years in 1985.

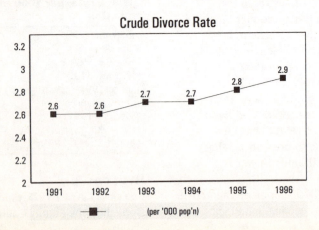

- About 40% of first marriages are terminated by divorce. As couples are having their children later in their marriage, the chances of a divorce occurring before the birth of the first child have increased. The number of divorces involving children has decreased: from 62.7% in 1976 to 54% in 1993.
- In 1996 the median duration of the separation preceding divorce was 7.6 years.
- The median age at divorce in 1996 was 40.2 years for men and 37.4 years for women.
- Of the couples who were divorced in 1996, 8.4% had separated between two and four years of the marriage, 37% separated within the first five years, and 22% in the next five years.

Children and divorce or separation

The older children are at the time of a divorce the more difficult it becomes for them to maintain contact with both their parents.
- Approximately 88% of children whose parents have separated live with their mothers, most of whom have not remarried.
- 77% of children of broken marriages are living with only one adult.
- About 42% of children whose parents have separated are able to see the other parent at least once every two weeks. 36% see the other parent less than once a year.
- About 60% of children 0–4 years affected by divorce or separation see their non-residential parent at least once a fortnight.
- About 25% of children aged two or more have no contact with the non-residential parent.
- Only 42% of children of separated parents receive direct cash assistance from the other parent, and another 16% receive a little help with clothes, pocket money or school fees.

Divorce rates, per 1000 of population

Australia (1993)	2.7
Canada (1992)	2.7
France (1991)	1.9
Germany (1993)	1.3
Japan (1993)	1.5
New Zealand (1992)	2.6
Sweden (1993)	2.5
United Kingdom (1992)	3.0
United States (1992)	4.6

THE FAMILY

The household

There were 6 898 000 Australian households in 1996 compared with 5 628 900 in 1986.

Family size

Since 1976 there has been a very considerable decrease in the average size of the family, and an increase in couple-only families. As the population has aged there has also been an increase in single-person households. People are living longer in couple-only families because they are having children later in life and are living longer.

◗ In 1976 60% of families were couples with children; this had dropped to 51% in 1996.

◗ In June 1994 the most common household type contained only two persons aged 15 years and over (32%). The next most common family type was the single-person household (23%).

◗ Only about 3% of people aged 15–24 years lived alone and 20% lived in two-person households. 32% of persons aged 65 years and over lived alone and 55% lived in a two-person household.

◗ 11.8% of the population living alone in 1996 were women and 9.7% were men.

◗ The mean average household size in 1996 was 2.7 persons per household. The family size had declined since 1991, except in the NT which had an average of 3.2 persons per household.

Couple families
Since 1991, the number and proportion of couple families with dependent children has declined from 44.2% of all families to 40.6%.

Lone-person households
In the period 1991–96 the number of lone-person households increased by 26.7%.

Lone-person households, 1996

	%
NSW	22
Vic.	22
Qld	21
SA	25
WA	22
Tas.	24
NT	17
ACT	21
Australia	**22**

For one-parent families with dependent children, as a proportion of all families, 8.4% had a female head and 1.3% a male head.

One-parent families, 1996

	% of all families
NSW	15
Vic.	18
Qld	15
SA	14
WA	13
Tas.	15
NT	16
ACT	15
Australia	**14**

Step- or blended families
There are 164 200 step- or blended families in Australia, containing 363 800 children. Step-families are the 4% of Australian families with one parent bringing up children from an earlier marriage. Blended families are the 3% of Australian families containing children from more than one relationship.

Families and the workforce
In June 1996 there were 1 798 000 families with children aged 14 years and under.

- 7.9% of these families had both parents unemployed, 37.7% had one parent employed and 54.4% had both parents employed.

Work and childcare
Use of childcare by employed parents
The work commitments of parents, and in particular of the mother, are linked to the use of childcare.

- 47% of children in 1996 were in families with both parents (or the lone parent) working.
- For all children under 12 years with both parents (or the lone parent) working, 71% of families used childcare.
- For all children under 12 years with both a parent working part-time and the other parent also employed, 60% used childcare.
- For all children under 12 years with one parent unemployed, 24% used childcare.

Informal care
The principal reason given for using informal care was related to the parent's work (47%), with parent's personal reason being given for 41% of children.

Cost and type of care
The cost of care depended to a very considerable extent on the type of care.

- 86% of the children who used childcare did so at no cost.
- It cost $60 or more per week for 31% of children attending long-day care and for 24% of those at family day-care centres. For children attending preschool facilities the cost was less than $20 per week.

Family income and use of childcare
As the family income increases there is also an increase in the number of children who use childcare.

- 43% of children in families with a weekly family income of less than $400 used some form of care.

- Attendance at childcare centres is a reflection of the increasing proportion of families with both parents working. In families with a family income in excess of $2000 a week, 75% of children are in some form of care.

Childcare Cash Rebate

The Childcare Cash Rebate (CCR) is a non-means-tested payment to families for work-related childcare costs that exceed $16.50 per week. The take-up rate for CCR increases with family income. Families with an income of less than $400 per week had a take-up rate of 44%, families with an income of $1500–$1999 had the highest take-up rate of 70%.

Children in supported placements

Children are placed in supported placements for a range of reasons pertaining to their care and protection, including abuse and neglect, illness of parents, or the inability of parents to provide proper care. These placements may be voluntary or under care and protection orders.

- As at 30 June 1997 there were 13 965 children in supported placements, 2785 of whom were Aboriginal or Torres Strait Islander children.

Retirement

The means-tested (based on income and assets) Age Pension is payable to men over 65 years of age and women over 60 years and 6 months.

The minimum qualifying age for women was established on 1 July 1995, and will be increased by six months at two-year intervals until 1 July 2013 when it will be 65 years of age.

Aged care

In 1993, the proportion of the Australian population aged 70 years and over was 7.8%. By 1998 it is estimated it will be 8.6%, by the year

2000 8.8% and by 2007 9%. The long-term projection is that by the year 2041 16.4% of the Australian population will be aged 70 years and over.

- There were about 132 500 residents (permanent and respite) in residential care facilities in June 1997: 72 500 in nursing homes and 60 000 in hostels. The number of persons in residential care increased by 12.7% between 1992 and 1997.
- Commonwealth government funding for long-term residential care services was about $2.7bn in 1996; the clients also contributed $685m.
- Commonwealth government expenditure on residential care services Australia-wide, per person aged 70 years and over, was an average of $1703 in 1996–97, with the highest being the NT at $2168, and the lowest in the ACT at $1312.

Indigenous aged-care recipients

Indigenous people tend to require aged care services at an earlier age than the general population.

- Participation for 1997 was measured against all indigenous people aged 50 years and over.
- The use of aged-care services by indigenous people was highest in WA (78.1 per 1000 indigenous people) and lowest in Tas. (17.6 per 1000 indigenous people).

People with a disability

The most recent ABS Survey of Disability, Ageing and Carers carried out in 1994 estimated that 15.6% of the population had a disability, i.e. a restriction or lack of ability to perform an activity at a normal level.

- 2.1% of people aged 5–64 years were affected by a severe disability whereby they sometimes required personal help or supervision.
- 2.9% were profoundly disabled, whereby they always required personal help or supervision.

Area of disability, as % of population aged 5–64 years

self-care	6.9
mobility	12.7
communication	3.3
schooling	1.1
employment	10.4

People with disabilities, 1994

	% of total population
Australia	**15.6**
Canada	15.5
France	9.3
Germany	8.4
Italy	9.3
New Zealand	13.0
Sweden	12.0
United Kingdom	14.2
United States	12.0

Financial assistance for people with a disability

There is a range of government-funded or provided services available to people with a disability, including the Commonwealth/State Disability Agreement (CSDA), the Home and Care Community program and the Commonwealth Rehabilitation Service.

◗ In 1995–96 the nominal government expenditure under CSDA was $1703m.

Labour force participation of people with a disability

In 1993 Australia's labour force included 54.9% of people with a disability who were of working age; 45.1% were employed.

Accommodation support for people with a disability

In 1996 61.9% of people with disabilities who were provided with accommodation support were receiving community-based care or support.

Community services

In Australia community services are provided by a large range of organisations. In 1995–96, 8036 businesses and organisational employers provided community services, with a total expenditure of $9.7bn.

Major areas of community services expenditure, 1995–96

	$m
residential care and accommodation support	5062
personal and social support	1525
childcare	1043

In 1996–97 childcare services, accommodation for the aged, residential services, non-residential care services and nursing homes had 80 542 full-time employees and 176 507 part-time. In addition these organisations depended on the services of 255 426 volunteers.

Government involvement in community services

About 5% of the employing businesses and organisations providing community services in 1996 were government service providers.

▶ Not-for-profit organisations were responsible for 54% of direct service expenditure in 1995–96, with for-profit institutions making up a further 19%.

▶ In 1996–97 total government expenditure on Home and Community Care was $762.4m, of which the Commonwealth government share was 61.7%.

Business/Organisations with Community Service Activities
Non-Government Sector
June 1996
28.11 — Profit Organisations
71.89 — Non-Profit Organisations

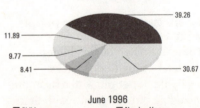

Community Services Industries
Non-Government Sector
June 1996
39.26, 30.67, 8.41, 9.77, 11.89
■ Childcare ■ Nursing Homes
■ Accommodation for the Aged ■ Residential Care Services
■ Non-Residential Care Services

Source of income, selected community service industries, 1995–96

	%
government funding	53
service to clients and other organisations	27
donations	5
sale of goods	5
other income	10

▸ Commonwealth expenditure per person aged 70 years and over in care was $2133 in 1996–97.

Ownership of residential facilities

As at January 1997, there were 74 406 places in nursing homes and 63 145 places in hostels.

▸ 14% of nursing-home places were in government ownership.
▸ 48% were in the hands of private enterprise.
▸ 38% were operated by religious or charitable organisations.
▸ In the case of hostels, 5.6% were in government ownership, 6.7% were owned by private enterprise and 87.7% were run by religious or charitable organisations.

RELIGION

Aboriginal and Torres Strait Islander religion

For the traditional Aborigine all features of social living were associated with religion through the interweaving of ritual and myth. Aboriginal religion was not identical throughout Australia, as each society had its own social integrity and had limited interaction with other groups. Two common features were the bond with the land and the concept of the 'Dreaming'. The advent of Christianity into Aboriginal communities had varying effects. In some areas the traditional religion has been virtually eliminated by the teachings of various Christian denominations. In other places, such as Elcho Island, the people have attempted to combine Christianity with Aboriginal traditional beliefs and practices.

Christian religions

The first Christian service was conducted by the Rev. Richard Johnson at Sydney Cove on 3 February 1788. The Anglican Church was the only authorised Christian denomination until 15 May 1803, when the first authorised Roman Catholic mass was held in Sydney by Father James Dixon, a conditionally emancipated convict. There are at least 270 distinct religious groups among the present population, many being small sects or groups, which are continually changing in number and/or persuasion.

In 1901, 74% of the population stated that they were Protestants, 23% Roman Catholics and about 50 000 affiliated to non-Christian faiths. Little change occurred in the proportions of religious affiliation until the large influx of migrants post–World War II. Since the 1971 census respondents have been able to state 'no religion' if they wish to.

- Anglicans have been replaced as the largest Christian denomination in recent years, partly due to recent migration from predominately Catholic countries.
- From 1981 to 1991 Pentecostal affiliation grew by 108%, the Baptists by 47%, Jehovah's Witnesses by 44.4%, Catholics by 21.7% and Anglicans by 5.7%.
- There has been a steady increase in the percentage stating that they have no religion, from 6.7% in 1971 to 12.9% in 1991. In 10.2% responses the religion was not stated. At the 1996 census 16.48% stated that they had no religion and the religion, if any, was not stated in 8.67% of responses.
- Based on the 1991 census returns 8% of nominal Anglicans, 18% of nominal Uniting Church affiliates, 31% of nominal Lutherans and 47% of Baptists are frequent church attenders.
- 19% of attenders of all Protestant

churches on an average Sunday are in Pentecostal churches.

▶ During the 1950s **about 40%** of the population **attended** church at **least once a month**; in the 1990s that figure has fallen to about 25%.

▶ In 1997 there were slightly over 10 000 priests, brothers and nuns in the Catholic religious orders in Australia, compared with more than 15 000 in 1981. The number of Mercy Sisters has decreased in the last 10 years from 2675 to 2034. The number of Christian Brothers (NSW Province) has declined from 259 in 1978 to 162 in 1998.

At the 1996 census 12.58 million persons stated that they were Christians, 26.82% were Catholics, 21.8% were Anglicans, 7.46% belonged to the Uniting Church, 3.77% to the Presbyterian and Reformed Church and 2.78% to the Orthodox Church.

▶ Among the states and territories NSW had the highest percentage of Christians with 74%, compared with a national figure of 70.32%. In SA 66% of the population said they were adherents of a Christian religion.

Non-Christian religions

In 1996 there were 548 400 members of non-Christian religions, representing 3.04% of the population, compared with 1.4% in 1981. Judaism has remained a small and stable religion at 0.4% of the population.

▶ Members of the Buddhist faith numbered 199 800 in 1996 (42.9% growth rate).

▶ Hindus numbered 67 900, up 54.4%.

▶ There were 200 900 adherents of Islam, up 36.2%.

▶ 79 800 were members of Judaism, having increased in numbers by 7.6%.

LANGUAGES

Aboriginal languages

Prior to the European arrival Aboriginal people were characterised by their great variety of languages. Although there were relationships between them, 200–300 separate languages and about 600 dialects were spoken. More than half these languages are now extinct. Fifty have 100 or more speakers and only 12 have more than 500 speakers. Only 10% of Aborigines now speak their own language and only 20 languages are actively transmitted and used by their children. The main languages still in substantial use are Pitjantjatjara, Tiwi, Walmatjari, Aranda and Wik–Munkan.

◗ 40 700 people use an Aboriginal language at home.

◗ It is estimated that only 10 Aboriginal languages will have survived in the next 30–40 years unless immediate and adequate

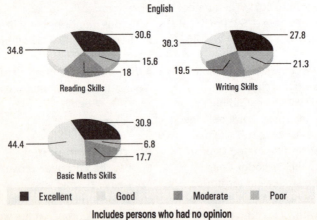

Self-rating Skills (by First Language Spoken) 1996

English

Reading Skills: 30.6, 15.6, 18, 34.8

Writing Skills: 27.8, 21.3, 19.5, 30.3

Basic Maths Skills: 30.9, 6.8, 17.7, 44.4

■ Excellent   ■ Good   ■ Moderate   ■ Poor

Includes persons who had no opinion

measures are taken to sustain Aboriginal languages.

▶ Two new Aboriginal Creole languages have evolved. Cape York Creole is used on the Torres Strait islands and in Qld Aboriginal communities, and Kriol is used across northern Australia.

Non-English languages

More than 60 languages, other than English, were used in Australian households in 1991 by 1 743 700 non-English speaking people. 52 100 people born in Australia spoke a language other than English at home.

▶ In the 1996 census 1 015 862 people in NSW and 816 558 in Vic. reported that they spoke a language other than English at home. Sydney (26.2%) and Melbourne (26%) of the

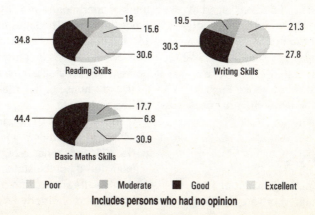

Self-rating Skills (by First Language Spoken) 1996

Other Languages

Reading Skills: 18, 15.6, 30.6, 34.8

Writing Skills: 19.5, 21.3, 27.8, 30.3

Basic Maths Skills: 17.7, 6.8, 30.9, 44.4

Poor ▪ Moderate ▪ Good ▪ Excellent

Includes persons who had no opinion

capital cities recorded the highest levels of people speaking a language other than English at home.

◗ The NT had 22.5% of people speaking a language other than English at home, the majority of whom (70.9%) spoke an Aboriginal language.

◗ There were 2 487 073 persons aged over five years who spoke a language other than English.

Proficiency in English

When asked in the 1996 census about their level of proficiency in English 52.05% of persons, aged five years and over, spoke English only. Of those whose mother tongue was not English, 19.72% said they spoke English very well, 16.29% spoke English well, 9.02% spoke English 'not well', and 0.57% did not speak English at all.

HOUSING

On census night 1996, out of 6.49 million occupied private dwellings, 2.67 million were fully owned, 1.66 million were being purchased and 1.86 million were being rented.

◗ There were 17 267 825 persons living in occupied private dwellings.

◗ The 1996 median weekly rent was $123, compared with $109 in 1991.

Dwelling structure

On census night 1996, 14.13 million people were living in separate houses, 1.06 million in semi-detached, row, terrace houses, or town houses, 1.44 million in flats, units or apartments, and 261 892 in other dwellings. The latter included 161 420 in caravans, cabins and houseboats, 27 464 in improvised homes, tents or sleep-outs, and 73 008 in a house or flat attached to a shop, office, etc.

◗ The total of 6 496 071 occupied dwellings included 84 595 in caravan parks, 1734 in marinas, 6243 in manufactured home estates, and 45 817 in self-care accommodation for the retired or elderly.

Tenure type of private dwellings
Of the 7 175 237 private dwellings reported on census night 1996 37.04% were fully owned by the occupiers, 22.66% were being purchased, 0.41% were being purchased under a rent/buy scheme.

Bank housing loan rates
The standard variable rate loans of large banking house lenders averaged 17% in 1988–89, 10.5% in 1991–92 and 7.55% in April 1997.

▶ The median monthly housing loan repayment in 1997 was $780, and it was $561 in 1991.

Household consumption of water
Domestic consumption of water (12%) is second only to its use for irrigation (70%). Much of household water is used for outdoor purposes, e.g. 30% in Sydney, 38% in Melbourne and 56% in Adelaide.

▶ The average household consumption was 500 kL per year with an average annual rainfall of 1659 mm.

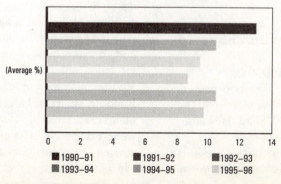

Housing Bank Loan Rates

(Average %)

■ 1990–91   ■ 1991–92   ■ 1992–93
■ 1993–94   ■ 1994–95   ■ 1995–96

- In Melbourne consumption was 270 kL per year with an average annual rainfall of 656 mm.
- Average consumption was 265 kL in Adelaide with an average annual rainfall of 451 mm.

Household expenditure on mortgage payments

In 1993–94 the average household spent $14.00 per week on the repayment of the principal of its mortgage.

Change of residence

As at February 1998, 19.9% of the population (2.67 million) had moved in the last 12 months.

1994 Australian housing survey

Bedrooms (in 000s)

344.4 dwellings were bedsitters or had one bedroom, 1568.5 had two bedrooms, 3513.4 had three and 1251.6 had four or more.

Bathrooms/en suites (in 000s)

18.4 residences had no bathroom, 5042.3 had one and 1617.2 had two or more.

Laundries (in 000s)

746.3 dwellings had no laundry and 5931.6 had one or more.

Separate toilets (in 000s)

1709 dwellings had no separate toilet, 4456.3 had one and 512.7 had two or more.

Lounge/dining rooms (in 000s)

140.2 had no lounge or dining room, 3563 had one, and 2973.8 had two or more.

House insulation (in 000s)

The need to conserve energy and the desire to reduce both heating and cooling costs has led to a greater demand for insulation. 2017.2 homes had fibreglass batts as roof insulation, 607.2 had loose fill and 366 used sisalation or reflective foil.

Building structural faults (in 000s)

Major cracks in walls and floors were reported in 210.6 cases, sinking or moving foundations 118.5 cases, sagging roofs and floors 109.4 cases, and walls out of plumb 63.9 cases. Rising damp affected 60.0 dwellings.

Most common housing problems (in 000s)

The most common problems reported relating to dwellings were pests (excluding termites) 1983.2 cases, electrical faults 1729.3 cases, draughts 1339.5 cases and mould and/or mildew 1199.9 cases.

Housing affordability

In the December quarter of 1997, the loan repayment required for a typical first-home mortgage was 17.6% of average household income compared with 18% at the same time the previous year and 21.5% two years previously. The median price for the typical house has continued to rise in most capital cities 1996 to 1997.

▶ These rises ranged from 21.4% in Sydney and 15% in Melbourne, down to 0.4% in Canberra. Prices fell 1.3% in Hobart.

1997 house prices, monthly median

Sydney	$280 000
Melbourne	$195 000
Brisbane	$142 000
Adelaide	$115 000
Perth	$140 000
Hobart	$116 000
Canberra	$145 000
Darwin	$176 000

Indigenous housing

For indigenous households, 63.8% were renters in capital cities, 76.6% in other urban areas and 62.5% in rural areas. For the same areas the percentages of indigenous households which were purchasers were 20.5%, 9.3% and 7%, and households that owned their houses 13.4%, 11.4% and 13.4% in the respective areas.

▶ Throughout Australia 26.1% of landlords of properties rented by indigenous households were from the private sector, 20.9% were rented from community organisations, and

46.4% from state housing and other government organisations.

◗ Reported rents were relatively low at an average weekly rent of $76. Some 60% of households were paying less than $77 a week.

Public and community housing
Public rental housing

In 1997 there were approximately 360 000 public housing dwellings in Australia i.e. 4% of all dwellings.

Households residing in public rental housing, 1996

	%
NSW	6.0
Vic.	3.8
Qld	4.5
SA	10.5
WA	5.6
Tas.	7.9
NT	18.9
ACT	10.5

◗ Total government spending on the provision of public rental housing was approximately $1.9bn in 1995–96. The Commonwealth/State Housing Agreement (CSHA) funding for public rental housing assistance totalled $1 061 951m, with the Commonwealth contributing about 66%.

◗ 64% of tenants of public housing in 1997 stated that they were either satisfied or very satisfied with their accommodation.

Community housing

In June 1996, there were about 24 600 community housing dwellings, representing about 6% of the total public housing stock. The Commonwealth and state and territory governments provide funding for community housing, which may include several models.

◗ Regional housing associations, which provide property management services and support services for tenants.

◗ Community groups managing housing stock owned by housing authorities.

- Housing partnerships involving church, welfare and local government agencies in joint venture equity arrangements with government.
- Housing cooperatives incorporating tenant management and maintenance, with the housing stock owned by government, a central finance company or individual cooperatives.

Public housing applicants waiting for less than one year

	%
NSW	21
Vic.	19
Qld	55
SA	31
WA	47
Tas.	69
NT	45
ACT	69

HEALTH

Since 1976 Australia has had a compulsory, universal, fee-for-service national health insurance scheme. It was known as Medibank at first, becoming Medicare in 1984. Medical services are provided by either private medical practitioners on a fee-for-service basis, or by medical practitioners employed in hospitals or community centres.

Medicare

The *Health Insurance Act* provides for a Medical Benefits Schedule, which lists a schedule fee applicable for each medical service provided by legally qualified medical practitioners, approved dentists and optometrical consultations by optometrists. Benefits are payable at the rate of 85% of the schedule fee for the services.
- In 1994–95 an average of 10.4 Medicare services were processed per person.
- Medicare benefits expenditure per capita was $330.05 in 1995–96, compared with $284.21 in 1992–93 at current prices.

- The average annual per capita value of Medicare benefits in 1994–95 was $288.85 for males and $406.55 for females.
- People aged 60 years and over used an average of 18.7 services per person; those aged 20–54 years used 6.7 services; and those aged less than 20 years used 6 services.

Health care expenditure

For the 1994–95 year the total health expenditure was $33 905m or $2145 per person. As a proportion of GDP health expenditure was 8.4%. Health expenditure by the Commonwealth government was $26 339m or $1468 per capita.

- The rate of growth of expenditure on health was 4% in 1994–95, compared with 5.4% in 1989–90.
- The Commonwealth and states fund over 80% of the expenditure on public hospitals, medical services and pharmaceutical benefits.

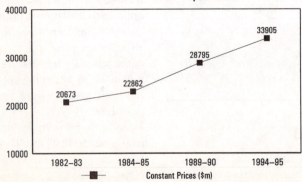

Growth in Health Expenditure

Selected areas of health expenditure, 1993–94

	%
recognised public hospitals	26.1
private hospitals	6.4
nursing homes	7.2
medical services	18.9
dental services	5.0
benefit paid pharmaceutical	6.2
other (includes capital items)	30.2

Household expenditure on medical care and health expenses

In 1993–94 the average couple with dependent children spent $43.32 per week on medical care and health expenses. A couple only with the reference person aged over 65 years spent $27.99 per week.

Bulk-billed and patient-billed services

In 1995–95 the average patient was $3.98 out-of-pocket per service for bulk-billed and patient-billed services compared with $4.08 in 1992–93 at current prices.

Health services expenditure

% paid by public insurance, 1991	
Australia	**70**
Canada	82
France	75
Germany	92
Japan	87
New Zealand	90
Sweden	94
United Kingdom	93
United States	61

	% of GDP, 1995
Australia	**8.4**
Canada	9.5
France	9.9
Germany	9.6
Japan	7.2
New Zealand (1990)	7.4
Sweden	7.7
United Kingdom	6.9
United States	14.5

▶ In 1995–96 71.1% of Medicare services were bulk-billed compared with 65.1% in 1992–93.

Private health insurance

The number of persons covered by

private health insurance has steadily declined, from 7.78 million in 1984 to 6.15 million in 1996. The percentage of the population covered in 1984 was 50%, falling to 33.6% in 1996. Ancillary cover is offered by the health funds for benefits not covered by Medicare, including private dental services, optical, chiropractic, podiatry, home nursing and other services. As at 30 June 1996 33.6% of the population was covered for health insurance only, 26% for health insurance plus ancillary cover and 7% for ancillary cover only.

Hospitals
Public hospitals

There were 702 public acute care hospitals in Australia in 1993–94, with an average of 56 140 beds available on any day. In addition there were 30 public psychiatric hospitals with 5106 available beds. In 1985–86 there were 4.1 hospital beds (excluding beds in public psychiatric hospitals)

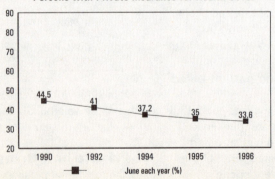

Persons with Private Insurance for Health Cover

per 1000 of population. This ratio had fallen to 3.2 for acute care beds per 1000 of population by 1993–94.

In 1993–94 there were 261 admissions per 1000 of population and the average length of stay was 4.8 days.

Private hospitals

In 1994–95 there was a total of 453 private hospital facilities. Occupied-bed days for private acute care and psychiatric hospitals totalled 5.4 million and the average length of stay was 4.1 days. 37 344 staff were employed in private hospitals, of whom 58.7% were nursing staff.

▶ Total operating costs of private acute and psychiatric hospitals were $2503m, with 59.1% expended on salaries and wages. Revenue received was $2763m.

Same-day surgery

There has been an increased use in recent years of same-day surgery, which has resulted in a marked decline in the average length of hospital stay. In 1992–93 the proportion of same-day patients in public hospitals was 31% and 39% in private hospitals.

▶ The average operating expenditure per patient was $369 in 1994–95. The average cost was highest for ophthalmic clinics at $669 and lowest for specialist endoscopy clinics at $218.

Private medical practice industry

During 1994–95 there were 11 933 general practice medical businesses employing 20 825 medical practitioners, and 10 364 specialist medical practices with 13 161 medical practitioners. 72 147 other persons were also employed. The gross income was $7240.9m, with an operating profit before tax of $1850.3m the year ended 30 June 1995.

Pathology services

For the year ended 30 June 1995 the pathology services industry had an operating profit before tax of $29.8m and an operating profit margin of 16.1%.

▶ 3020 persons were employed in the pathology industry, 63% in full-time employment.

Ambulance services

The number of incidents in 1995–96 for which ambulances turned out ranged from 682 200 in NSW to 15 000 in the ACT, with patients being transported in 66% of responses in Vic. and 75% of responses in NSW.

▶ Ambulance services in the states and territories cost more than $540m in 1996–97, with the per-person expenditure being the highest in Qld at $41 per person and the lowest in Tas. at $26 per person.

▶ Funds for ambulance services come from transport fees, subscribers to insurance funds and some state and government subsidies.

Pharmaceutical benefits

The Pharmaceutical Benefits Scheme (PBS) provides Australians with a considerable range of required medicines, as prescribed by medical and dental practitioners. The patient, depending on his or her circumstances, may pay as little as $2.70 and need not pay more than $17.40 for any prescription, with the Commonwealth government meeting the rest of the cost. The 'safety net' provision operates to provide financial protection for high users of medicines, and comes into operation for most families when their expenditure on prescriptions reaches $600 per annum, thereafter the charge is set at $2.70 for additional PBS items for the remainder of the calendar year. In 1995–96 the total cost of the scheme was $2669m, including $478.1m from patients' contributions towards the cost of prescriptions.

▶ In June 1996 there were 3539

pharmacies in urban areas and 1370 in rural areas. The total of 4954 was a decline of 45 from 1994–95. Australia-wide there were 3725.6 persons per pharmacy.

Significant pharmaceutical drug groups by Commonwealth government cost

During 1995–96 the drug group with the highest cost to the Government was the antacid category (drugs for treatment of peptic ulcer and flatulence). There were 7 356 937 scripts, which cost the government $269.7m. The total cost of the drugs was $308.1m and the average price per script was $41.89.

▶ The most prescribed drug was paracetamol 500 mg tablet, with a script volume of 3 754 416, at an average cost of $7.50 and a total cost of $29.9m.

Health industry employment

In 1995–96 there were about 268 800 persons employed in health occupations, comprising a little over 3% of the total of those in employment. There were 71 300 males and 197 500 females. The largest section of those in the health workforce were the 160 500 nurses, of whom 92.3% were females. There were also 30 800 general practitioners, of whom 75% were males, and 15 000 specialist practitioners, of whom 77.3% were males.

▶ In 1997 there were 230 doctors per 100 000 of population.

Selected health conditions
Asthma

Asthma is characterised by extreme narrowing of the airways as a response to a spectrum of stimuli, and is usually associated with an allergic response to environmental agents. Asthma is one of the most chronic diseases in Australia and affects about 10% of the population.

Between 1979 and 1985, the mortality rate for asthma rose from 3 to 5.2 per 100 000 of population. Since 1985, the rate has stabilised.

Prostate cancer

Each year about 4000 Australian men are diagnosed as having prostate cancer; over 1600 will die from the condition.

Breast cancer

Breast cancer is the most common cause of cancer death for females.

- 2629 women died from breast cancer in 1995, i.e. 4% of all female deaths. This is a rate of 29 per 100 000 women.
- The average age for the diagnosis of breast cancer is 64 years. Eight women per 100 000 aged between 25–45 years died of breast cancer in 1995 compared with 215 per 100 000 women aged 85 and over.

Children's health

In 1995 61% of children had undertaken a recent health action.

- 51% had used a medication.
- 19% had consulted a doctor.
- Children aged 0–4 years were more likely to have undertaken a health action than those aged 5–14 years.

Infectious diseases

During 1995, of the notifiable diseases reported, there were 4380 cases of rubella (German measles), 4297 cases of whooping cough, 1324 cases of measles and 153 cases of mumps.

Immunisation

In 1995 68.6% of children were fully immunised against diphtheria, 59.9% against whooping cough, 82.6% against poliomyelitis, 91.6% against measles, 89.6% against mumps, 75.5% against rubella and 50.2% against hamophilus influenzae.

Lead in children

Several Australian cities, e.g. Port Pirie (SA), Broken Hill (NSW) and Wollongong (NSW), experience severe atmospheric pollution from lead smelters. Sydney often has heavy atmospheric pollution from vehicle exhausts. Environmental, airborne lead is recognised as playing a significant role in the impaired cognitive development of young children.

Sun protection

Sun protection measures, in children aged 0–14 years, 1995

	%
none	12.8
hat	79.7
sunscreen	63.7
protective clothing	49.4
sunglasses	19.9
umbrella	4.5
sun avoided	24.9

Gender health differences

In 1998 the ABS reported that the average Australian man receives 8.7 Medicare services a year, whereas the average woman receives 12.4. Men are more likely to smoke, consume alcohol in amounts considered to be a health risk and as a whole spend longer periods in the workforce, with men predominating in the more hazardous occupations.

Selected male and female health condition rates per '000 people

	males	females
short-sightedness	180.3	225.9
hayfever	130.7	147.4
arthritis	121.9	170.1
deafness	126.4	66.1
asthma	108.2	117.7
hypertension	105.0	107.9
headache	106.7	153.2
sinusitis	84.2	121.5
common cold	53.1	61.0
allergy	48.9	72.7

General health and well-being

A National Health Survey conducted in 1995 showed that three-quarters of the population took one or more health-related actions in the fortnight prior to the survey, with the use of medications being the most common action.

- An estimated 30% used vitamins/minerals or natural/herbal remedies and 59% used other medications.
- About 20% of males and 26% of females had consulted a doctor.
- Compared with the previous survey in 1989–90 the 1995 survey showed a move towards healthier lifestyles and non-traditional health procedures.
- The proportion of adults who smoked (24%), did little or no regular exercise (63%) or who drank alcohol at medium or high-risk levels (8%) were lower in 1995 than in 1989–90.
- The percentage who were overweight or obese (35%) was down on the 38% in 1989–90.

Drug abuse
Alcohol

In 1992 the hazardous and harmful consumption of alcohol was responsible for 2521 male deaths (3.85% of all male deaths) and 1139 female deaths (2% of all female deaths). There were 71 593 hospital episodes and 731 169 bed-days attributed to alcohol.
- In 1995 46% of women and 66% of men reported that they had drunk alcohol in the previous week.
- 6% of men and 15% of women said that they never drank alcohol.

Tobacco

Habitual tobacco smoking represents a risk factor for heart disease, stroke, lung cancer and chronic lung disease. It has been estimated that active smoking resulted in 18 920 Australians dying in 1992 and also led to 98 373 hospital episodes and 812 866 hospital bed-days. Since 1945 the Australian smoking rate has declined dramatically for males. Women have always had a lower smoking rate than men but the gap has narrowed in recent years. Total tobacco consumption rose from 1965 to the mid-1970s and has declined slightly since.

▶ A Morgan Research Centre public survey in 1995 found that 28.2% of males smoked, down from 30.7% in 1991, and that 24.7% of women smoked, down from 26.1% in 1991.

▶ There were 13 857 male deaths (21% of all male deaths) and 5063 female deaths (8.8% of all female deaths) attributed to tobacco in 1992.

▶ The per capita annual consumption of loose tobacco has declined from 4.71 kg in 1987 to 1.78 kg in 1965. In the same period the consumption of cigarettes has risen from 22.07 kg to 26.3 kg.

▶ In 1986 smokers averaged 20 cigarettes a day compared with 17 in 1965.

▶ In WA smoking was estimated to cause more deaths than alcohol among indigenous and non-indigenous people alike.

Smoking by Australian school children

A study in 1993 found that among 12-year-olds, 8% of boys and 6% of girls had smoked in the last week and that among 16-year-olds, 32% of boys and 35% of girls had smoked in the last week.

International smoking rates

A 1990 survey of 39 countries ranked Australia sixth for the per capita annual consumption of cigarettes, at 2703, on a list that ranged from Cyprus at 4831 to Papua New Guinea at 24.

Tobacco taxation

As at 3 February 1997 federal excise duty and state licence fees totalled $4.21 on a pack of 25 cigarettes retailing at $6.53 and $4.71 on packs of 30 retailing at $7.21. In 1995–96 federal excise totalled $185m and state licence fees $2622.3m.

Household expenditure on tobacco

In 1993–94 the average household spent $9.42 on tobacco per week.

Adults who smoke, 1986–94

	males (%)	females (%)
Australia	37	30
Canada	31	28
France	49	26
Greece	54	13
Japan	66	29
Sweden	36	30
United Kingdom	36	32
United States	30	24

State and territory taxes on alcohol and tobacco

Franchise taxes remain a very significant source of state government revenue, despite state-sponsored anti-smoking campaigns, rising from $994m in 1990–91 to $2622m in 1995–96. Liquor franchise taxes have experienced a more modest increase in the same period: $603m to $735m.

Illicit drugs

In 1992 there were 384 male deaths related to the use of illicit drugs (0.65% of all male deaths) and 104 female deaths (0.2% of all female deaths). There were 5390 hospital episodes and 40 522 bed-days attributed to illicit drugs.

▶ A survey of 3500 persons in 1993 found that 13% had used marijuana, 2% had used amphetamines, and 1% had used ecstasy/designer drugs in the previous 12 months.

▶ The use of illicit drugs may cause psychotic effects and drug dependency. The unborn child may also be harmed by the mother's use of drugs.

▶ 95% of the deaths ascribed to use of illicit drugs were caused by opiates (including injecting drug use).

Illicit drug seizures by Australian Customs

During 1996–97 the Australian Customs Service made 1620 seizures of illicit drugs: 998 of cannabis, 49 of cocaine, 62 of heroin, 78 of ecstasy and 384 of other substances. 349 of the seizures were from air passengers and 176 were postal interceptions.

- The weight of cannabis seized rose to a very high level at 24 295 kg, compared with 53.3 kg in 1995–96 and 6514.64 kg in 1994–95.
- Seizures of cocaine totalled 67.5 kg in 1996–97, compared with 58 kg the previous year.
- The quantity of heroin seized ranged from 294.4 kg in 1994–95 to 64.3 kg the following year, and 169 kg in 1996–97.
- The quantity of ecstasy seized has grown significantly, from 5.7 kg in 1994–95 to 31.4 kg in 1995–96 and 74.7 kg in 1996–97.

Petrol sniffing

Petrol sniffing is a serious problem in Aboriginal communities, particularly among boys, and especially in the NT. An NT Government report estimates that there are about 200 sniffers located in 10 remote Aboriginal communities.

Drugs and sport

In 1994–95 the Australian Sports Drug Agency conducted 394 international drug tests on Australian athletes. There were 25 positive results indicating the presence of banned substances, including 14 for stimulants, one for a narcotic analgesic and seven for anabolic steroids.

Indigenous health

When indigenous people were asked for their perception of health problems, they placed alcohol at the top (57.9%), followed by drugs (29.7%), diabetes (21.6%), diet/nutrition (19.3%) and heart problems (13.7%). About 93% perceived alcohol consumption and about 92% alcohol-related violence as major health and social problems.

Causes of death

In 1992–94, three out of every four deaths among indigenous people resulted from diseases of the circulatory system (heart attacks and strokes), injury and poisoning (road crashes, suicide and murder), respiratory diseases (pneumonia, asthma and emphysema), neoplasms (cancers) and endocrine, nutritional and metabolic disorders (diabetes).

◗ Indigenous death rates were higher than those of non-indigenous people for every age group, with the disparity being greatest in those aged 25–55.

Eye diseases

Aboriginal and Torres Strait Islander people suffer from blindness 10 times more frequently than do other Australians.

◗ In rural Australia the rate of blindness was 1.49% for Aboriginal people compared to 0.16% for non-Aboriginal people.

◗ More than 20% of Aboriginal children under 10 years in rural areas have follicular trachoma.

Cataract

Professor Fred Hollows was a pioneer in providing eye surgery to restore the sight of Aboriginal and Torres Strait Islander people afflicted by cataracts.

◗ There is an overall prevalence of lens abnormalities among 3.6% of Aboriginal people compared to 0.8% among non-Aborigines.

Diabetes

Diabetes is a major health problem for Aboriginal and Torres Strait Islander people: in many communities 8–13% of people are affected.

◗ These people are all at risk of developing diabetic eye disease, which may lead to blindness.

Breast cancer

A 1998 national survey conducted by the National Breast Cancer Centre found that although indigenous women had a lower incidence of breast cancer than non-indigenous women, they were more likely to die from it.

SOCIAL SECURITY AND WELFARE

The Commonwealth government introduced its first age pension on 1 July 1909 and this was followed by the invalid pension on 15 December 1910.

Age pension

The age pension is paid to men who have reached 65 years. For women the pension was paid at 60 years and 6 months from 1 July 1997, with the qualifying age to be increased by six-monthly increments until the limit of 65 is reached in 2013.

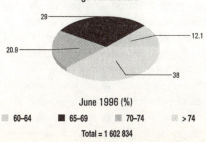

Age Pensioners

29
12.1
20.9
38

June 1996 (%)

60–64   65–69   70–74   > 74

Total = 1 602 834

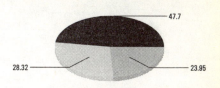

Disability and War Widow Pensioners

47.7
28.32
23.95

June 1996 (%)

■ Incapacitated Veterans   ▨ Dependents of Incapacitated Veterans
▧ Dependents of Deceased Veterans

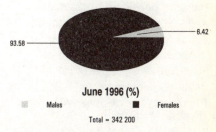

Sole Parent Pensioners

6.42
93.58

June 1996 (%)

Males   ■ Females

Total = 342 200

The rate of the pension is now fixed at 25% of average adult weekly earnings. The amount of pension paid to individual recipients is subject to the

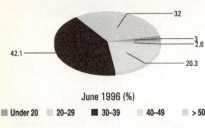

Sole Parent Pensioners

June 1996 (%)

- Under 20
- 20–29
- 30–39
- 40–49
- > 50

pensioner's level of income and assets. As at 30 June 1996 there were 1 602 834 people receiving the aged pension: 570 328 males and 1 032 506 females. The total outlay for the year was $12 283.9m. A pharmaceutical allowance of $5.20 fortnightly is paid to all qualified pensioners.

Payments for people with disabilities and the sick

A range of benefits is paid to people with disabilities and the sick, and in special circumstances to carers. The total cost of these benefits for the year ended 30 June 1996 was $4917.4m.

Family Payment

The Family Payment was paid for dependent children under 16 years and dependent full-time students, aged 16–18 years, who were not eligible for a Prescribed Education Scheme payment such as AUSTUDY. In June 1996 payment was made in respect of 3 497 467 children. Other payments in respect to families with children include the Maternity Allowance, Parenting Allowance, Sole Parent Allowance and Double Orphan Allowance. Payments in 1995–96 totalled $5877.6m.

In 1998 the Commonwealth government introduced the Youth Allowance which applied (a) to full-time students aged 16–24 years, (b) to unemployed people aged under 21 years looking for work or combining part-time work with job search, or undertaking any other approved activity, or temporarily incapacitated, (c) independent

15-year-olds above the school leaving age (e.g. homeless).
- To be eligible a young person must be an Australian resident or have served a newly arrived migrant waiting period of 104 weeks.
- The Youth Allowance is subject to a parental income test, and a family asset test.

Superannuation

Prior to the 1990s superannuation was a benefit available to only a limited group of occupations and industries. The Superannuation Guarantee Charge introduced in 1992 had the intention of extending superannuation coverage to all employees and to progressively increase the level of contributions.

Persons covered by superannuation

There were 6 545 100 employed persons for whom superannuation provisions were in place in November 1995, i.e. 81% of all those employed. These workers were contributing to a superannuation scheme and/or their employer or business was making a contribution to a scheme on their behalf.
- 87% of full-time workers and 62% of part-time workers were covered by superannuation in November 1995.
- In the same year 82% of male workers and 79% of female workers were covered.
- 95% of public sector and 88% of private sector employees were covered by superannuation.
- 97% of permanent employees were covered compared with 65% of casual workers as a whole and 59% of casual part-time employees.
- More employees who were members of a trade union were covered by superannuation, at a rate of 97%, than non-members at 85%.
- Among those aged 45–74 years 98% of those earning $600 and over a week were covered, compared with 56% of those earning $200 per week

and 88% earning between $200 and $400 per week.

Persons not covered by superannuation schemes

As at 30 November 1995, 3 072 800 employed persons aged 45–74 were not covered by superannuation. 70% had ceased full-time work, 18% had not ceased full-time work and 12% had never worked full-time or had not decided whether or not they would work full-time in the future.

▶ 531 100 employed persons aged 45–74 years were not covered by a superannuation scheme. 31% were not making personal contributions as they considered the cost too high or could not afford it. 13% had not bothered, had never considered making personal contributions or were not interested.

Contributions to superannuation savings

Personal contributions were compulsory for 34% of the 45–74 age group. Males contributed an average of $55 per week compared with females at $40 per week.

Retirement payment arrangements

Of all those aged 45–74 years covered by superannuation at 30 November 1995, 1 328 652 (68%) expected to receive a lump-sum payment from their superannuation schemes, 11% did not anticipate receiving a lump sum and 21% did not know whether they would receive a lump sum.

Number and assets of superannuation funds

By June 1996 there were about 140 000 superannuation entities, comprising 137 000 superannuation funds, 2700 approved deposit funds and 295 pooled superannuation trusts.

▶ The largest 1300 funds in 1996 held about 85% of assets. Only 4% of funds had assets in excess of $1m and 77% of funds held less than $250 000.

▶ In June 1997 superannuation funds had total assets of $185 792m, compared with $134 450m in 1995.

The largest forms of statutory funds were equities, units and trusts (35.04%), long-term securities (21.15%), assets overseas (12.9%) and short-term securities (11.21%).

People in poverty

In Australia the Henderson Poverty Line (HPL) is used as a measure of the proportion of the total line of people said to be in poverty. In 1995–96, the HPL was set at a net income of $496 or less for a family of 2 adults and 2 children.

People in poverty, per '000 of population, 1995–96

income units	1825
people	3412
children	1026

FOOD AND NUTRITION

Estimates of the apparent consumption of foodstuffs are compiled by deducting the quantity exported from the local production and imports.

Beverages

Tea

Australians are drinking less tea: in 1968–69 they used 2.5 kg per capita, compared with 0.9 kg in 1995–96.

Coffee

Australians have become heavier drinkers of coffee. In 1968–69 they consumed 1.2 kg per capita; by 1995–96 it had risen to 2.2 kg.

Aerated and carbonated waters

There has been a steady growth in the consumption of carbonated beverages, and to a lesser extent cordials and syrups: 47.3 L per capita were drunk in 1968–69 and 114.6 L in 1995–96.

▶ Expenditure on soft drinks in 1996 included $2260m on cola, $170.8m on sports drinks and $145.8m on still water.

Beer, wine and spirits

In recent years there has been a

marked change in Australian beer drinking habits, due in part to the introduction of low-alcohol beer and to the effects of breath analysis of motorists. In 1984–85 the per capita consumption of beer was 114.5 L, of which 12.9 L was low-alcohol beer. By 1995–96 the per capita consumption was 95.3 L. The apparent consumption of low-alcohol beer was 22.4 L per capita in 1995–96, an increase of 4.6% on the previous year.

Australians have also shown an increasing appreciation of the many high-quality wines now available. Wine consumption remained steady at 18.3 L per capita in 1995–96, having risen from 17.9 L per capita in 1990–91. In the late 1940s wine intake per annum was 5.9 L per capita.

◗ There has been a very substantial decline in the consumption of spirits: from 8.59 L per capita in 1984–85 to 1.16 L in 1994–95.

◗ If 1989–90 is taken as the base of 100, the 1995–96 price index for alcoholic drinks is 128.6 for beer, 123.5 for wine, and 130.0 for spirits, compared with the consumer price index of 118.7.

◗ The average weekly household expenditure on alcoholic beverages during 1993–94 was $17.46.

Milk (fluid)

The annual per capita consumption of milk has remained almost constant since the 1980s – the average for 1988–89 was 101 litres. In the 1990s there has been a slight overall increase in consumption of milk, being 102 litres in 1993–94 and 104.2 litres in 1995–96.

Solid food
Butter, table margarine and cheese

The consumption of butter and table margarine has changed dramatically. The 1968–69 consumption per capita was 9.8 kg of butter and 1.5 kg of table margarine. By 1994–95 butter consumption had fallen to 2.9 kg per capita, and in 1995–96 the figure was 2.5 kg. The consumption of dairy spreads has increased to 0.8 kg per capita. The annual per capita consumption of cheese has risen from 3.5 kg in 1968–69 to 10.6 kg in 1995–96.

Red meat and meat products

Australians have been eating less red meat. The annual per capita consumption of beef/veal, mutton/lamb and pig meat was 87.4 kg in 1969 and 71.7 kg in 1995–96. In that period the consumption of beef and veal fell from 38.6 kg per person to 36.7 kg, lamb and mutton fell from 37.7 kg to 17 kg, and pig meat rose from 11.3 kg to 18.1 kg.

Eggs and poultry

Australians are consuming fewer eggs. In 1968–69 they consumed the equivalent of 222 eggs per capita; this had fallen to 132 in 1992–93. There has been a continued, steady rise in consumption of dressed poultry, from 10.5 kg per capita in 1969 to 28.3 kg per capita in 1995–96.

Seafood

Australians are eating more seafood, including crustaceans and molluscs. In 1968–69 the consumption of seafood including shellfish was 5.6 kg per capita; by 1992–93 it was 8.3 kg. In 1995–96 Australians consumed 3.2 kg fresh and frozen fish per capita sourced from Australian waters and 1.9 kg of imported fish.

Fruit

The consumption of fruit has continued to rise from a total fresh fruit equivalent of 86.5 kg per head in 1968–69 to 122.1 kg in 1995–96. In the same period the consumption of jams, conserves, dried and preserved fruit fell from 5.2 kg to 2 kg, and the consumption of processed fruit fell 14.5% to 6.4 kg.

Vegetables

The fresh vegetable equivalent consumption per capita rose from 124.3 kg in 1968–69 to 162.8 kg in 1995–96.

▶ Potatoes, at 70.1 kg per head, were

by far the most heavily consumed vegetable in 1995–96, followed by leafy and green vegetables at 21.5 kg.

Cereals and cereal products

The annual per capita consumption of grain products (flour, breakfast foods, table rice, and other cereal products) rose from 86.8 kg per capita in 1968–69 to 93.1 kg in 1995–96, in part reflecting the migrant influence on Australian dietary habits and the wider range of packaged cereal products.

▶ The per capita consumption of table rice has risen from 1.9 kg in 1968–69 to 6.5 kg in 1995–96.

Sugar and honey

The annual per capita consumption of refined sugar has dropped significantly. It was 51.9 kg per capita in 1968–69; by 1995–96 it had fallen to 46.6 kg.

▶ Sugar consumed in processed foods was 27.7 kg per capita in 1968–69 and 36.5 kg in 1992–93.

▶ Australians continue to use just under 1 kg honey per capita annually.

Ice cream and related products

In 1995–96 328 million litres of ice cream and related products were manufactured in Australia, compared with 309 million litres in 1991–92, with a production value of $1.28bn.

Household expenditure on food and non-alcoholic beverages

In 1993–94 the average weekly household spending on food and non-alcoholic beverages was $111, representing 18.26% of the total family expenditure.

EDUCATION AND TRAINING

The state and territory governments have the major responsibility for education, including the funding and administration of primary, secondary and technical and further education (TAFE). The Australian education system has two elements at the primary and secondary levels, with schools being administered by state/territory governments or by non-government organisations, almost all of the latter being associated with various religious bodies.

Government expenditure on education

About 55% of government spending on education in 1994–95 was on primary and secondary education and 35% on tertiary education. Over a period of six years government outlays on tertiary education increased by 45%, whereas at the same time the increase in expenditure on primary and secondary education rose 22%. The Commonwealth government has a significant role in setting educational policies, programs and funding.

▶ Total expenditure by governments on education was $23bn in 1994–95, representing 5.6% of GDP.

▶ State and territory governments fund the transportation costs of students who are at a stated distance from their schools. In 1994–95 $180m was spent on transportation.

Preschool education

All states and territories, except NSW, have a policy of making preschool attendance universally available for children in the years prior to entry into the school system. The Commonwealth government has little input into the preschool system. In 1996–97 the Commonwealth government outlaid $85m on preschool and special education, whereas the state, territory and local governments contributed $1170m. The participation rate in 1996 ranged from about 97% in Qld to 83.3% in the NT. Attendance fees are not usually charged in those states where preschools are government-run, but in others fees may be payable to private or voluntary organisations.

▶ In 1996 there were 258 394 children attending preschool.

Compulsory primary and secondary education

Attendance at primary or secondary schools is compulsory throughout Australia between the ages of six and 15 years, except in Tas. where the upper age limit is 16 years. The states and territories are responsible for curriculum development in their schools, with the Commonwealth government promoting equity and social justice policies and encouraging national cooperation in curriculum development. There was a total of 9630 schools operating in Australia in August 1996: 7088 (73.6%) were under the control of state Departments of Education and 2542 (26.4%) were non-government schools. There had been a decrease of 34 in government schools and an increase of 16 non-government schools since August 1995.

Primary schools
Student enrolment

As at August 1996 3 143 015 full-time students were enrolled at these schools, 2 221 557 (70.7%) at government schools and 921 458 (29.3%) at non-government schools.

▶ Full-time students attending government schools increased by 13 704 (0.6%) between August 1995 and August 1996. For the same period the attendance at non-government schools increased by 19 974 (2.2%).

▶ On census night 1966 there were 1 737 569 children attending primary schools.

Students attending non-government schools

In 1995 of the children attending non-government schools, 67.5% were at Catholic schools, 9.9% were at Anglican schools, 4.5% were at Uniting Church schools and 2.2% at Lutheran schools.

School fees

In 1993–94 the average student fees per week in government primary schools were $2.00 and $24.78 in non-government primary schools. At the secondary school level the average weekly fees per student were $4.81 in government schools and $75.78 in non-government schools.

Staffing resources

In August 1996 full-time and part-time teaching staff in all schools totalled 223 432 persons, or 203 972 full-time equivalent units (FTE).

▶ There was an FTE increase of 162 (0.1%) in government schools, and an FTE increase of 1409 (2.4%) in non-government schools.

▶ The number of students per FTE was about 15 in both government and non-government schools, being 18 for primary and 13 for secondary schools.

▶ In 1975 59% of teachers were female, while by 1995 64% were female.

Attainment in mathematics and science

The Third Mathematics and Science Study in 1994 studied the attainment in mathematics and science of over half a million students at three stages of their schooling. The same tests were used in 45 countries around the world and in more than 30 languages. In Australia at the first test level in some states the children tested were Years 3 and 4, but Years 4 and 5 in other states. The schools were selected at random.

▶ At Years 4 and 5, only six countries outperformed Australia in mathematics and only two countries scored better in science.

▶ At Years 3 and 4, only four countries were better than Australia in mathematics and only one performed better in science.

▶ WA students performed best in the world in science – equalled only by those from South Korea.

Secondary education
Participation in post-primary education

In September 1996 there were 1 358 300 Australians aged 15–24 years attending an educational institution, representing 51% of the 15–24 population. In 1991 48% of the 15–24 age group were involved in education.

- 694 800 15–24 year olds were attending school, 370 100 were attending higher education institutions and 240 500 were at TAFE.
- 52 900 were at business colleges, industry skills centres or other institutions.
- Between 1991 and 1996 participation of 15–24 year olds in tertiary education grew from 22% to 25%.
- 685 300 males and 672 900 females aged 15–24 years were in educational institutions.
- The ACT (59%), Vic. (55%) and NSW (53%) had participation rates higher than the national average of 51%.
- In September 1996, 49% of 15–24-year-olds born in Australia were attending an educational institution, compared with 60% of those born overseas.

Apparent retention rates

In 1996 the apparent retention rate of secondary school students to Year 10 was 96.3% for males and 98.2% for females. In Year 11 it was 80.4% for males and 84.4% for females. By Year 12 it was 66.2% for males and 77.8% for females.

- In 1992 the apparent retention rate of students in Year 12 was 72.5% for males and 82.0% for females. These rates had fallen to 65.9% and 77.0% respectively in 1997.
- In 1997 for government schools the retention rate for Year 12 was 65.7% for all students; in non-government schools the rate was 84.8%.

Age of leaving school

At the 1996 census, 101 027 persons aged 15 years and over indicated that they had never attended school,

1.90 million left school at 14 years and under and 523 864 at 19 years and over.

Commonwealth government assistance to students
AUSTUDY

AUSTUDY was a means-tested scheme providing financial assistance to secondary and tertiary students aged 16 years and over.

◗ The scheme commenced in 1987, when 225 000 students received the benefit; the number of students had increased to 485 026 in 1996.

◗ AUSTUDY expenditure was $151m in 1995.

The conditions for AUSTUDY were revised in 1998. Students under 25 years of age are now covered by the Youth Allowance. To be eligible for AUSTUDY a student must be 25 years and over, with conditions applying similar to those of the Youth Allowance, with the additional restriction that the student is not receiving other government assistance for study.

ABSTUDY

The basic conditions of eligibility for this allowance are the student must be (a) an Australian Aborigine or Torres Strait Islander according to the Commonwealth definition of Aboriginality, (b) studying an approved course at an approved educational institution and (c) not receiving other government assistance to study. ABSTUDY is subject to a personal income test and an assets test.

◗ ABSTUDY assisted approximately 45 800 students in 1995 for an expenditure of $119m.

Assistance for isolated children (AIC)

AIC provides financial assistance for families of primary, secondary and in some cases tertiary students who, because of geographic isolation, disability or other reason, e.g. the family being itinerant, are not able to attend an appropriate government institution.

▶ 12 064 students were assisted by AIC in 1995 for an expenditure of $23m.

School of the Air

In addition to correspondence lessons there is provision for children to receive tuition from the School of the Air, which was founded in 1951 by Molly Ferguson, using the Royal Flying Doctor Service based at Alice Springs.

Higher education

The University of Sydney, inaugurated on 11 October 1852, was Australia's first place of higher learning. In 1995 there were 36 public and one private institution (Bond University, Qld) recognised by the Australian Vice-Chancellors Committee. Higher education institutions are self-governing independent entities generally administered by councils.

Funding is primarily the responsibility of the Commonwealth government. Contributions are also received from students through the Higher Education Contribution Scheme (HECS), either as up-front fees or indirectly as deferred payments.

There were 604 177 students attending higher education institutions in 1995. The 1996 census showed that 6% of the people in Australia were taking part in study, either full-time or part-time, in Technical and Further Education (TAFE) institutions, universities or other tertiary institutions.

Male/female ratios in higher education

In 1990 there were 229 420 male and 278 820 female students enrolled in higher education courses. In 1995 there were 278 820 males and 325 357 female students.

▶ In 1995 there were 204 363 male and 250 483 female enrolments at the Bachelor degree and at the postgraduate qualifying/preliminary diploma. Graduate Certificate level female students outnumbered male students 28 951 to 21 155.

▸ At the Higher degree level (Doctorate/Master's degrees) there were 40 549 males and 33 470 females.

▸ In 1997 female students represented a record of 54.4% of enrolments in higher education.

Women continued to dominate in the humanities and also made inroads into formerly male-dominated areas, including business, law and architecture. Female enrolments increased by 14 400 over the previous year, whereas male enrolments fell by 10 300.

Fields of study

In 1987 the three most popular fields of study were Arts, Humanities and Social Sciences (95 714 students), Business, Administration and Economics (72 688) and Education (72 112). In 1995 there were 139 367 students in the Arts, Humanities and Social Sciences (up 45.6% since 1987), 129 177 in Business, Administration and Economics (up 77.7%) and 88 172 in Science (up 71.5%).

▸ 70 635 were studying Education in 1995, a decline of 2% from 1987.

▸ In the same period the number of students studying in the health field had increased from 37 328 to 72 137 (up 93.3%).

▸ The 1997 enrolment figures for tertiary education showed a shift by female students into subject areas traditionally male-dominated. There was a rise of female participation in business-oriented degrees of 11.9%, 10% in law degrees and 5.4% in science degrees.

Enrolment status of students

In 1995 of the total student enrolment of 604 177, 87.55% were internal and 12.45% were external students. Of the 528 979 internal students 67.16% attended full-time and 32.84% part-time.

Age of students

In 1995 the 20–24 age group, with 32.28%, was the largest age group represented in higher education.

Aboriginal and Torres Strait Islander students

In 1996 there were 6956 Aboriginal or Torres Strait Islander students attending higher education institutions or 1.1% of all students – an increase of 2.2% over 1995.

Size by enrolment of higher education institutions

Of the 44 higher education institutions there were three with more than 30 000 students enrolled, Monash University (Vic.) with 39 516 being the largest.

▶ 14 institutions had enrolments of between 10 000 and 19 999 students.

▶ Marcus Oldham Farm Management College (Vic.), with 86 students, had the lowest enrolment.

Staffing in higher education institutions

There was a total of 78 766 staff in higher education institutions in 1996.

▶ 33 313 (42.9%) were in the academic classifications and 45 453 (57.1%) in the non-academic classifications. In 1988 total staff numbers were 64 137.

Starting salaries for graduates

In 1996 students graduating in dentistry and medicine had an average starting salary of $40 000, in earth sciences and optometry $35 000, engineering $32 500 and computer science $30 000.

Open learning

Distance learning in Australian higher education began in 1911 when the University of Queensland first offered correspondence courses. A pilot project was launched in 1992 to trial an 'open university' using television as the medium of learning. Open Learning Australia (OLA) was established and now has a consortium of nine universities headed by Monash University. OLA has offered university education to many mature-age students and to females with home responsibilities.

▶ 29 universities and TAFE colleges were involved in the OLA program in 1995.

▶ In 1993 there were 4854 students of OLA, including three Aboriginal and Torres Strait Islander students.

▶ In 1996 there were 7735 students of OLA, including 41 Aboriginal and Torres Strait Islander students, compared with a peak total of 9057 students in 1994.

▶ 8% of the 1995 OLA students were aged under 19, 25.5% were aged 20–25 and 66.5% were over 25. For students taking a conventional university education the corresponding figures are 27.3%, 35.5% and 37.2%.

Aboriginal and Torres Strait Islander education
Primary education
In 1996 there were 64 857 Aboriginal and Torres Strait Islander children in primary schools; 89.26% were in government schools and 10.74% in non-government schools. Of the latter, 8.02% were in Catholic schools. Boys outnumbered girls by 1361.

Secondary education
There were 27 810 children in secondary schools, 84.31% at government schools and 15.72% at non-government schools. 5.19% were at Catholic secondary schools. Girls outnumbered boys by 208.

▶ In Year 8 in 1996 there were 7120 Aboriginal and Torres Strait Islander pupils, by Year 10 the figure had fallen to 4932, in Year 11 it fell to 2855 and by Year 12 there were 1741 remaining.

Overseas students
Australia's participation in international educational services was part of its foreign policy/foreign aid program until the mid-1980s. In 1986 there were 20 000 international students in Australia sponsored by government or aid-based programs.

Since that time there has been an Australian government change to an emphasis on private, full fee-paying students. At the end of 1995 it was estimated that the number of full fee-paying overseas students annually had risen to 80 720.

◗ In 1994–95 there were 66 465 long-term and 205 742 short-term arrivals for education purposes. Of total arrivals, 15 340 were from Indonesia, 12 454 from Malaysia, 11 050 from Singapore, 10 689 from Hong Kong, 9474 from Korea and 9237 from Japan.

◗ 9760 overseas students were in schools, 46 520 in government-funded universities, 7300 in private higher-education institutions, 3230 in TAFE colleges and 8230 in English Language Intensive Courses (ELICOS).

◗ Overseas students paid $1710m in fees and living allowances while studying in Australia in 1994–95.

◗ In 1994–95, there was a total of 604 177 overseas students in Australia, 278 820 males and 325 357 males; 355 284 were full-time, 173 695 were part-time and 75 198 were external (i.e. correspondence) students.

Overseas students in higher education

In 1995 there were 51 944 overseas students studying in Australian higher education institutions.

◗ 75.14% of the overseas students came from Asia and the Middle East, 5.4% from the Pacific Islands and 3.12% from the Americas and the Caribbean. 13.95% were studying Business Administration and Economics, 14.81% Science and 12.29% Arts, Humanities and Social Sciences.

Vocational education and training (VET)

There were 1124 training provider locations administering and/or delivering vocational education and training in 1995. The majority were TAFE colleges and some were libraries, community centres or churches. NSW and Vic. provided 71% of all VET institutions and 65% of TAFE vocational enrolments.

- There were 659 772 male and 587 909 female vocational education and training clients in 1995.

Apprentices

In recent years there has been a decline in the number of apprentices in training. There were 160 989 in 1990 and 133 542 at 30 June 1995.

- For male apprentices the most popular field of training was building (26 171), followed by the motor-vehicle trades (19 501) and the electrical trade and electronics (15 659).
- For female apprentices hairdressing was the most popular trade (8924), followed by the clerical trade (4426) and the food trades (3385).

Employer-based training

As at 30 June 1995 there were 133 542 persons undertaking training through contract or training arrangements, including apprenticeships, Australian Traineeship System trainees and other forms of employer-based training. There were 111 531 males and 22 011 female trainees.

Technical and further education (TAFE)

TAFE institutions provide a wide range of vocational and non-vocational training programs, including basic employment and educational preparation for the trades, para-professional and professional levels, as well as recreation and leisure courses.

- 1995 recurrent funding for the TAFE system was $3400m, of which the Commonwealth government contributed 23%, the states 59% and fees and other charges 18%. Most students paid some form of administration fee.

Vocational education and training clients

In 1995 there were 1 272 681 clients, most of whom were enrolled in TAFE institutions, 51.83% being male and 41.17% female.

▶ In the September quarter of 1996 17.77% of employers provided structured training, compared with 22.62% in the same period of 1993.

▶ Employers expended $185.49 per employee on training in the September quarter of 1996, compared with $191.25 in the same period of 1993.

Educational attainment of persons aged 15–64

In May 1995 40.97% of Australians aged 15–64 had a post-school qualification, 17.65% had completed the highest level of school, 36.02% did not complete the highest level of school and 5.28% were still at school.

▶ 1.52% of 15–64-year-olds had a higher degree, 1.95% had a post-graduate degree, 8.41% had a bachelor's degree and 9.13% had an undergraduate/associate diploma. 13.47% had skilled vocation qualifications and 6.44% had basic vocational qualifications.

People with university degrees, 1996

	%
NSW	11
Vic.	12
Qld	9
SA	9
WA	10
Tas.	8
NT	10
ACT	23
Australia	**10**

LABOUR

The workforce

In April 1997 there were 8 413 000 people in the Australian workforce; of these 2 060 000 were females (24.5%).

▶ In April 1989 80 300 were employed at home. By September 1995 this had increased to 343 300.

Participation rate

The April 1997 participation rate in the workforce for the population aged 15 years and over was 63.5%, with males at 73.3% and females at 54.1%.

Status in employment

Within the labour force in 1995–96 there were 363 900 employers, 849 100 own-account workers, 6 998 900 employees and 75 400 contributing family workers.

Workforce characteristics, 1996 annual average of workforce 15 years and over

	Participation rate (%)	Unemployment rate (%)
Australia	**74.7**	**8.5**
Canada	75.9	9.7
France	67.8	12.4
Germany	70.3	9.0
Italy	58.5	12.0
Japan	77.3	3.4
Sweden	79.0	8.0
United States	79.3	5.4

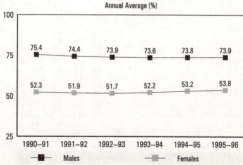

Participation Rates
Annual Average (%)

	1990–91	1991–92	1992–93	1993–94	1994–95	1995–96
Males	75.4	74.4	73.9	73.6	73.8	73.9
Females	52.3	51.9	51.7	52.2	53.2	53.8

Employed persons by specific industry groupings

The industry with the highest proportion of employed persons during 1995–96 was the retail trade (14.8%), followed by manufacturing (13.4%). Property and business services employed 9.6%, whereas agriculture, forestry and fishing employed 5.1%.

Employed persons by occupation

During 1995–96 10.6% of persons employed were managers and administrators, 14.1% were professionals, 5.7% were para-professionals, 14.4% were tradespeople, 16.4% were clerks, 16.9% were salespersons and personal service workers, 7% were plant and machine operators and drivers, and 14.9% were labourers and related workers. 42% of salary and wage earners were employed in the private sector and 58% in the public sector.

Full-time and part-time workers

For 1995–96, 89% of males in the

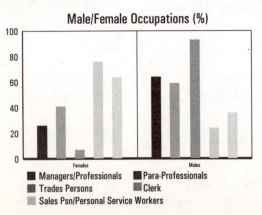

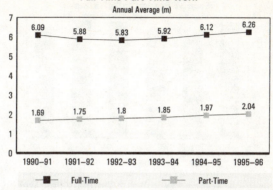

workforce were working full-time and 11% part-time; for females 57.5% were full-time and 42.5% were part-time workers.

Hours of work

In November 1994 males worked an average of 40.8 hours per week, and females 29.3 hours. For the year ended May 1996 the average total weekly earnings for full-time non-managerial employees was $683.00, an increase of 4.2% on the previous year. Males earned $729.70 (up 4.6%) and females $605.70 (up 3.2%). The largest percentage increase was in government administration and defence.

Overtime work

During the year ended May 1996 average weekly overtime earnings for male non-managerial employees was $207.00 compared with overtime earnings for females at $113.40. Males were paid for a weekly average overtime of 8.3 hours and females 4.8 hours.

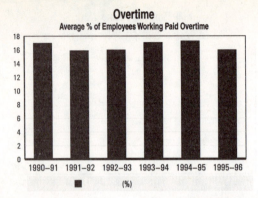

Work at home

In September 1995 it was estimated that 26% of those in employment worked some hours at home, an increase of 11.5% since March 1992.

▶ 230 700 females were employed at home compared with 112 600 males.

Average weekly earnings of full-time employees

For 1995–96 the average total weekly earnings for all persons was $557.30, males earning $664.30 and females $557.30.

▶ Ordinary time weekly earnings for full-time adults: the male rate was $705.10 and the female rate was $585.80.

▶ Total weekly earnings (including overtime) for full-time adults was $761.90 for males and $599.90 for females.

▶ In the 12 months to May 1997 full-time ordinary earnings for males and females rose by 3.7% and 4.3% respectively, and adult total earnings rose by 3% and 4.2% respectively.

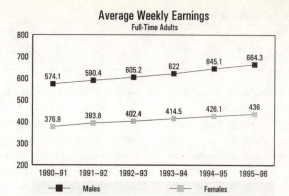

Changes in wages and prices (%)

	12 months to January 1997	10 years to January 1997
average full-time weekly earnings, adults	4.0	58.6
CPI all groups	−0.2	40.4

Personal income

In 1991 the median weekly personal wage for those aged 15 years and over was $268 (about $13 936 p.a.); at the time of the 1996 census it was $292 ($15 184 p.a.).

▶ The highest median weekly personal income in 1996 was recorded in the ACT at $430, followed by the NT at $358.

▶ The lowest average median income levels were Tas. ($257) and SA ($267).

▶ For the capital cities the highest median incomes were Canberra ($430) and Darwin ($426), and the

Weekly household income, 1996

($)								
AUS	NSW	VIC	QLD	SA	WA	TAS	NT	ACT
637	655	643	618	553	657	530	850	904

lowest levels were Adelaide ($273) and Greater Hobart ($283).

Employment levels in the occupational groups

Between 1986–87 and 1995–96 personal service workers were the fastest growing occupational group (+91.3%), followed by business professionals (+89.9%) and medical and science technical officers and technicians (+85.8%). The miscellaneous clerks group was the fastest shrinking group (–41.3%), followed by construction and mining labourers (–41.3%) and metal fitting and machine tradespersons (–15.1%).

Job vacancies

In February 1997 there were 62 200

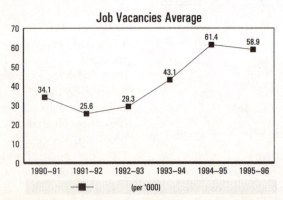

Job Vacancies Average

Year	Value
1990–91	34.1
1991–92	25.6
1992–93	29.3
1993–94	43.1
1994–95	61.4
1995–96	58.9

(per '000)

job vacancies in all industries, a rate of 76.8 job vacancies per 1000 unemployed. This compares with 130.3 in 1988–89 and 29.3 in 1992–93.

Labour costs

In 1993–94 Australia's total labour costs were $196 701m, up 10.9% since 1991–92. However, the amount of earnings paid to employees as a percentage of total labour costs had fallen to 88.4%, down from 89% in 1991–92 and 89.6% in 1986–87. The fall was the result of a large increase in superannuation costs. The proportional cost of superannuation rose from 4.9% to 5.6% of total labour costs.

▶ The total labour costs per employee in 1993–94 were $39 933 in the public sector and $30 022 in the private sector.

▶ The ACT had the highest costs per employee at $36 082 and Tas. the lowest at $29 311.

▶ The mining industry had the highest labour costs per employee at $67 140 and accommodation, cafés and restaurants the lowest at $18 569, principally because of the large number of part-timers and juniors employed in the industry.

Worker satisfaction with management

The 1995 Australian Workplace Industrial Relations Survey found that 46% of all employees were satisfied with the way management treated them, 26% were neither satisfied or dissatisfied and 26% were dissatisfied.

▶ 50% of all employees in the private sector were satisfied with the manner in which management treated them, compared with 39% in the public sector.

▶ 41% of private-sector employees agreed that management could be trusted compared with 30% in the public sector.

Commonwealth public sector employment

The present Commonwealth government made 77 400 public servants redundant in its first two years in power. The reduction of employees from 352 900 in February 1996 to 275 500 in November 1997 represented 21.9% of the total number of employees.

Unemployment

Since 1990 unemployment in Australia reached a peak in 1992–93 when the rate hit 11.7%. At April 1997 632 800 persons were looking for full-time work and 169 500 for part-time work. The unemployment rate was 8.7%.

▶ There were 55 000 persons aged 15–19 years looking for their first jobs.

▶ In December 1978 the unemployment rate for those aged 15–19 was 19.1%; in December 1995 it was 21.6%.

▶ The unemployment rate was 8.5% for those born in Australia and 9.8% for those born outside Australia.

Long-term unemployment

Long-term unemployment is the term used for those who have been unemployed for more than one year. As a proportion of total unemployment, male long-term unemployment at April 1997 was 32.3%, with the female figure at 28.5%.

Unemployment rate, annual average

1990–91	8.3
1991–92	10.3
1992–93	11.0
1993–94	10.5
1994–95	8.9
1995–96	8.5

Average duration of employment, weeks

1990–91	39.4
1991–92	45.5
1992–93	53.6
1993–94	57.5
1994–95	57.5
1995–96	51.7

Adults not in the workforce, 1996

	%
NSW	38
Vic.	37
Qld	37
SA	40
WA	35
Tas.	40
NT	30
ACT	28
Australia	**37**

Involuntary part-time employment

In September 1997, 546 500 (6%) of the 8.43 million employed persons aged 15 years and over were involuntary part-time workers. They worked less than 35 hours per week and would have preferred longer hours. The proportion of involuntary part-time workers as a percentage of all those employed rose from a low of 3.6% in 1989 to a high in 1992 and 1993 of 6.9%.

▶ About 91% of involuntary part-time workers usually worked part-time. The rest usually worked full-time for less than 35 hours because of economic reasons, such as insufficient work.

▶ 56% of involuntary part-time workers were female.

▶ 23% of involuntary part-time workers were aged 45 years and over in September 1996 compared with 17% in May 1985.

Job search experience

During the 12 months to July 1996 1 882 800 persons were successful in seeking a job. 748 200 were unsuccessful, down from the peak of 970 800 in the year to July 1992.

▶ 35% of those unsuccessful seeking a job in the year to July 1996 had spent the whole year looking for work.

Income support for the unemployed

As at June 1996, the Job Search Allowance (JSA) for those unemployed for less than one year, and the Newstart Allowance (NSA) for those unemployed for more than one year, were in operation. These allowances were amalgamated into a single payment under the JSA. For the year ended 30 June 1996, 240 907 males and 92 609 females received either JSA or NSA payments for a total cost for the year of $5.8bn.

◗ The Youth Training Allowance (YTA) was paid at AUSTUDY rates to unemployed people under 18 years.

◗ The Mature Age Allowance (MAA) was paid at pension rates to people who had been receiving income support and had no recent workforce experience. There were 46 037 MAA customers, payments to whom totalled $436.5m.

Voluntary work

A volunteer is someone who willingly gives unpaid help by way of time, service or skills through a formally structured group or organisation. In 1994–95 an estimated 2.6 million people, 19% of those aged 15 years and over, performed voluntary work. They spent about 430 million hours of their time in voluntary work.

◗ 25% of all volunteers were people aged 35–45 and 57% of all volunteers were women.

◗ Women aged 35–44 had the highest volunteer rate: 31% of all women in this age group engaged themselves in voluntary work.

Trade unions

The Sydney Shipwrights' Association, formed in 1829, is believed to be the first trade union set up in Australia. In December 1881 the Vic. Tailoresses' Union, the first union for women, was established.

◗ The Australian Labor Federation was formed on 11 June 1899 to bring all unions together; 10 unions were represented at the first meeting.

◗ On 3 May 1927 the Australian Council of Trade Unions (ACTU) was created as a trade union congress.

Number of trade unions

Changes in the labour force, and the amalgamation of two or more unions into larger single entities, has resulted in a decline in the number of unions. On 30 June 1996 there were 132 trade unions with a total membership of 2 800 500. This was 10 unions less than 1995, with seven unions merging into three larger unions. In 1950 there were 359 unions.

- In 1996 there were 12 unions with memberships of 100 000 and over, representing 71.2% of all trade union members. There were 21 unions with under 100 members.
- The average membership of unions was 166 178.

Female membership of unions

For a number of years there has been a steady increase in the proportion of women belonging to unions: in 1970 women made up 24.4% of members; by 1997 it had risen to 35%.

Permanent and casual employee union members

In August 1995 38.6% of permanent and 14.2% of casual employees belonged to unions.

Industry representation of union members

The industry group with the highest union membership in 1995 was the communications sector (66.1%), with lowest being agriculture, forestry and fishing (9.9%).

Industrial disputes

The first industrial dispute in Australia was probably in 1829 when compositors at the *Australian* newspaper struck to protest against a reduction in the real value of wages brought about by a currency devaluation.

- Qld shearers were on strike for five months in 1891; 12 unionists were convicted of conspiracy and sentenced to three months' gaol.

Number of disputes, 1991–96

1991	1036
1992	728
1993	610
1994	560
1995	643
1996	543

▶ The 1917 transport strike affected 95 000 workers and resulted in the loss of 4 689 300 working days.

▶ An internal airline pilots strike in 1989 caused chaos in the nation's transport system and tourist industry, and resulted in a restructuring of the employment of pilots on the major internal airlines.

▶ In 1991 there were 1036 industrial disputes, with a loss of 1 610 500 working days.

▶ During the 12 months ended January 1998, there were 439 disputes involving 313 200 employees, with 519 3000 working days lost.

THE CRIMINAL JUSTICE SYSTEM

Aboriginal people and law and justice

Many young Aborigines and Torres Strait Islanders come into conflict with the law; these encounters become more frequent as they grow older and are likely to set a pattern that may affect adult attitudes towards the legal system. In the June quarter of 1996 the average number of indigenous people in prison was 3316, 19% of all prisoners in Australia. The national rate of imprisonment of indigenous people was 18 times greater than the rate for non-indigenous imprisonment.

In 1993 17% of Aboriginal people aged 13 years and over needed to use legal services; of these, 67% used the Aboriginal Legal Service, 16% used Legal Aid and 13% used other legal services. The 25–44 year age group (22%) had the greatest need for legal services. Male need for legal help was 21% and female 13%.

- One in five of those aged 13 years and over had been arrested at least once in the last five years, 32% of males and 9% of females.
- Those who said they had been taken away from their natural parents as children had been arrested more often (22%) than those who had not been removed (11%).
- About 13% of those aged 13 years and over had been physically attacked or verbally abused in the previous 12 months. Only 44% of those attacked reported the incident to the police. 45% solved the matter themselves or knew the perpetrator and 23% did not want to involve the police, feared the police or disliked the police.
- Almost 10% of all Aboriginal people aged 13 years and over reported being hassled by the police in the previous year. 14% of males reported that they had been hassled, contrasted with 5% of females.

Deaths in custody

Aboriginal people are markedly over-represented in all forms of custody and there has been no change from the Royal Commission's final report into Aboriginal deaths in custody, tabled in May 1991. In 1996 Aborigines were 19 times more likely to die in custody than non-Aboriginal people. One of the determining factors of the higher rate of Aboriginal deaths in custody is the over-representation of Aborigines and Torres Strait Islanders in prisons. For the period 1990–96 there were 529 deaths in custody: 94 were Aborigines/Torres Strait Islanders and 435 non-Aborigines. In 1996 there were 80 deaths of prisoners aged 15 or more years in police custody, prison and juvenile detention; 17 of these were Aboriginal and Torres Strait Islander prisoners. Deaths in custody per 100 000 of population were 8.71 for

Aborigines/Torres Strait Islanders and 0.44 for non-Aborigines. Of those Aborigines who died in custody nine had been sentenced, three were on remand, and one was in protective custody.

▶ In 1996, 32 of the Aboriginal deaths were while in police hands, 62 were in prison and six while in a juvenile detention facility.

▶ Many of the Aborigines who died in custody were there for relatively minor offences, e.g. break and enter, motor-vehicle theft, drunkenness, property damage, drink driving and other traffic offences.

▶ Seven of the Aboriginal deaths were by hanging, five from natural causes and five from injuries.

▶ Four of the Aboriginal deaths from injuries occurred while in police custody.

Crime

An Australian Institute of Criminology 1997 report estimated the total cost of crime in Australia was a minimum of $10 410m.

▶ The total for homicide was $323m, assaults, including sexual assaults, $979m, robbery and extortion $37m, breaking and entering $1193m, fraud and misappropriation $3000m, theft of motor vehicles, boats and aircraft $654m, shoplifting $1020m, stealing from the person $545m, other theft $659m, property damage/environmental damage $2000m.

▶ It was not possible to estimate the costs of a range of other crimes, e.g. kidnapping, abduction, child abuse, hijacking, defamation, handling stolen goods, pollution and other environmental offences, good order offences, traffic offences. The report estimated the criminal justice system costs for 1996 were a maximum of $6433m.

Personal crime

Personal crime includes robbery, assault and sexual assault. In the year to April 1995, 540 000 persons were the victims of personal crimes, with the risk of victimisation being highest among the 15–24 years age group. In general the occurrence of personal crime was higher for males than females.

▶ 35.6% of personal crimes were robberies, 66.9% were assaults and 6% were sexual assaults.

Kidnapping/abduction

There were 479 victims of kidnapping/abduction in 1995, with females twice as likely than males to be the victims.

▶ 46.5% of the victims were females in the 0–19 years age group; 48% of kidnapping/abduction offences took place on the street/footpath.

Homicide

Homicide is the unlawful killing of another person and includes murder, attempted murder, manslaughter and driving causing death. In 1995 there were 351 cases of murder or manslaughter, a rate of 20 victims per 100 000 of population. In most cases a weapon was used. Males aged 20–24 are the most likely murder victims. A weapon is used in most murders and in 18% of cases a firearm is used.

▶ Someone known to the victim is responsible for the majority of murders committed.

▶ Murder most commonly occurs in a private dwelling.

▶ In 1996 the highest murder rate among the states and territories per 100 000 of population was the NT at 9.3, with Tas. having a rate of 7.8. The lowest rates were 0.3 in the ACT and 1.1 in WA.

▶ Males are killed by a firearm twice as frequently as females.

▶ People in the age groups 30–39 and 50–59 are more likely to be the victims of firearm-related homicide than those in other age groups.

Other unlawful killing

Manslaughter and driving causing death are the other forms of unlawful killing. Manslaughter is unlawful killing which takes place with no malice aforethought. During 1996 there were 37 victims of manslaughter and 339 victims of driving causing death offences.

Assaults

Nationally the police recorded 113 535 victims of assault in 1996, an increase of 12% between 1995 and 1996. Males aged 20–34 years make up most of the victims of assault and over half of the victims know their attackers. Assault offences most frequently occurred in private dwellings, with 34% of all assaults.

- Weapons were used in 10% of assault offences, with the use of firearms being 0.5%.

Robbery

Robbery entails the taking of property without consent accompanied by force or threat of force or violence and/or placing the victim in fear. In 1996 the police recorded 16 346 victims of robbery, an increase of 12% on 1995.

- In about a quarter of robberies organisations are the victims.
- Males are twice as likely as females to be victims of robbery.
- Retail locations are the most common locations for armed robberies, unarmed robberies are most common on the streets.
- The highest rate for armed robbery per 100 000 of population was in WA with 54.8 victims, and the lowest rate was Tas. (10.1) and the NT (10.5).

Firearms

Firearms were involved in 18% of murders and 27% of attempted murders in 1995, increases of 2% and 3% over 1994. There were several years in the recent past with marked increases in the number of multiple killings by firearms, usually brought about by a single assailant killing a number of people at random: 32 died in 1987, 11 in 1990, 10 in 1991, 20 in 1992 and 42 in 1995.

- In the period 1980–95 there were

6676 firearm deaths, 283 were accidents, 5487 were suicides and 813 were homicides.

- Handguns were used in 5.3% of all deaths involving firearms, shotguns in 30.2%, hunting rifles in 63.2% and military-style rifles in 1.3%.
- In suicides 54% involved the use of hunting rifles, for a further 24% a shotgun was used.
- Accidental firearm deaths in 1995 were at a rate of 0.2 per million of population, the rate for suicide firearm deaths was 2.1 and for homicides 0.3.
- In terms of premature mortality, firearm deaths in the period 1980–95 accounted for 2.4% of total years of potential life lost before 76 years of age.
- During 1996 there were 6217 victims of armed robberies, an increase of 18% on 1995.

Mass gun killings

In the period 1986–96 there were 11 mass gun killings in Australia, with the number of persons ranging from 35 in the Port Arthur (Tas.) mass shootings to five at Top End (WA). In addition 55 people were wounded in the shootings.

- In five cases the incidents involved a murder/suicide.
- Only one of the perpetrators had a previous criminal record, two had a previous history of mental illness, and all but one had a gun licence.
- 64% of the victims killed were victims of a shooting where a military-style weapon was used, with shotguns accounting for the remaining deaths.

Australian firearms buyback program

After the 1996 Port Arthur (Tas.) tragedy the Commonwealth and state/territory governments co-operated in the introduction of a weapons buyback scheme, with the owners being compensated and the firearms being destroyed.

- By 5 p.m. on 24 July 1997 469 341 firearms had been handed in at collection centres and $243.28m paid in compensation to the owners.

Sexual assault

In 1995 more than 80% of victims were female, over half were under 20 years and 40% were under 15 years. Sexual assaults most commonly took place in private dwellings and most of the offenders were known to their victims.

- In 1996 the police recorded 14 394 cases of sexual assault, up 11% from the 12 962 cases of 1995.
- The highest rates for sexual assault per 100 000 of population were NT (149) and WA (99.5). The lowest rates were in Tas. (33.7) and the ACT (35.1).

Women's experience of violence

A 1996 report found that 7.1% of all women in Australia had experienced violence during the last 12 months.

- For 6.2% of all women the perpetrator of the violence was male and in 1.6% of cases female. In some cases the woman may have experienced violence from both a male and a female.
- 4.9% had experienced physical violence and 1.9% had experienced sexual violence from a male perpetrator.
- 4.3% had experienced physical assault, 3.3% physical attempted assault or threat, 1.4% sexual assault and 0.7% sexual threat from a male perpetrator.
- 1.2% of women experienced physical assault and 1.3% physical attempted assault or threat from a female perpetrator.
- Women were nearly four times more likely to experience violence by a male than by a female.
- 19% of women aged 18–24 experienced an incident of violence in the previous 12 months, compared with 6.8% of women aged 35–44 and 1.2% of women aged 55 and over.

Household crime

The most common household crime was 'break and enter', which affected 333 700 households (5.3%) in the mainland states and the ACT in the 12 months to April 1995.

- About 8% of households were victims of either 'break and enter' or 'attempted break and enter'.
- 2% of households experienced at least one motor-vehicle theft.

Larceny in Australia

Larceny is defined as the wrongful taking and carrying away of personal goods of another with the intent permanently to deprive him or her thereof. It includes theft of motor cycles and bicycles. In 1972 the larceny rate per 100 000 of population in Australia was 1612.2, in 1982 it was 2084.4 and in 1995 it had risen to 2960.8.

Burglary

Burglary is the crime of breaking and entering with the intent to commit a felony. The Australian rate of burglary per 100 000 of population was 948 in 1972, 1496.3 in 1982 and 2131.9 in 1995.

Motor-vehicle theft

In 1972 the Australian rate of motor-vehicle theft per 100 000 of

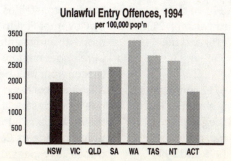
Unlawful Entry Offences, 1994
per 100,000 pop'n

population was 355.4, by 1982 it was 572.7 and in 1995 it was 703.
▶ It has been estimated that car theft cost Australia $809m in 1996, an increase of 24% on the previous year.
▶ During 1995–96 the states/territories with the highest rate of car theft per 1000 vehicles were WA (14.6) and NSW (14.2). Tas. and the ACT were the lowest at 8.1 and 8.4 respectively.
▶ In 1996 professional thieves were responsible for 55% of the costs of car thefts, petty thieves 23% and joyriding and vandalism 22%.
▶ In Vic. in 1996 the Holden Commodore was the most commonly stolen vehicle with 17% of claims, followed by the Ford Falcon (12%), the Ford Fairmont (6%) and the Mitsubishi Magna (3%).

Credit card crime

In 1996 there were 6717 complaints of credit cards being stolen or lost or PIN numbers used illegally. Unauthorised EFT transaction rose by 69.1% between 1995 and 1996.

Drug offences

During 1994, 54 815 arrests were made nationwide for drug-related offences, 46 491 (85%) were concerned with cannabis, 4593 (8.4%) with amphetamines, 2992 (5.5%) with heroin, 540 (1%) with LSD and 299 (0.5%) with cocaine.
▶ In 1994 there were 1569 prisoners who had been sentenced for drug offences, 145 for possession/use of drugs, 1211 for dealing/trafficking in drugs and 213 for manufacturing drugs.

The police

The first constables were appointed by Governor Phillip to protect property and maintain order. They were under military control and were chosen from well-behaved convicts. Australia now has eight police forces, one for each state and the NT, and the Australian Federal Police (AFP) which, beside its Commonwealth duties, is responsible for providing policing services in the ACT. The National Crime Authority (NCA) also has a policing role. The AFP has responsibilities for the prevention, detection and investigation of such matters as drug offences, laundering of money, organised crime, identifying the proceeds of crime and fraud against the Commonwealth. The NCA has the mission of counteracting organised criminal activities and to reduce their effect upon the Australian community, working in cooperation with other agencies.

Size of the police forces

At 30 June 1995 there was an Australian total of 42 517 sworn police officers, of whom 13.5% were female. Only 1% of female officers were of Inspector rank or above. NSW had one female Assistant Commissioner, as did the NT. The highest rank held by a female officer in WA was Senior Sergeant.

- There were 1563 gazetted police stations nationwide in 1994–95.

Police expenditure and salaries

Police total expenditure was $3.2bn in 1994–95, ranging from $1.1bn in NSW to $56.27m in the ACT.

Average annual police staff salaries ranged from $59 425 in Vic. to $44 085 in WA, with a nationwide average of $52 753.

Police work and health

Compared with some 40 overseas police populations, police shooting fatality rates in Australia are close to average. In comparison with the USA, the rates of death and wounds by guns of police officers throughout Australia are negligible. Many police officers are affected by the stress placed upon them, when dealing with the public and coping with distressing incidents, such as road and other accidents, and violent assaults and/or deaths.

People shot by police in the course of duty

Between 1 January 1990 and 30 June

1995 there were 32 deaths resulting from gunshots inflicted by police.

Police and public relations

In February 1997 it was reported that for all persons aged 18 years and over 67.6% of males and 68.7% of females were satisfied or very satisfied with the services provided by the police.

Courts

There are courts in all states and territories dealing with both criminal and civil cases. The court structure is hierarchical, with most of the less serious cases being dealt with by magistrates and the more serious before judges. Appeals are available from all levels of courts, with the High Court of Australia being the highest court of appeal for both criminal and civil matters. There are seven judges appointed to the High Court of Australia, which sits on constitutional disputes and can also hear appeals from all other courts. A High Court of Australia decision is final. There is also a national structure of Family Courts with the right of appeal to the High Court.

- In 1995 there were 153 Supreme Court judges, 206 District/Country court judges and 392 magistrates.
- 29 900 criminal matters were filed before the High Courts and 1.5 million before Magistrates' Courts. 766 900 minor traffic matters were also filed.
- 80 900 civil matters were filed in the Supreme Courts and 623 900 in Magistrates' Courts.
- The average court costs per criminal offender was $391.60, ranging from $555.30 in the NT to $204.50 in SA. The average costs per minor traffic offender was $18.30. The total expenditure on the courts system was $5241m in 1993–94, involving 5558 full-time staff.

Prisons

All states and the NT have prisons and other correctional services. Each state and territory makes provision for dealing with juvenile offenders. The ACT has a juvenile detention centre and a remand centre, with convicted adult prisoners being placed in NSW prisons, and local custodial provision being made for the short-term custody of remand prisoners and parole services. In NSW, Qld, SA and Vic. privately operated gaols have been established as part of the correctional services.

▶ There were 88 prisons operating in 1994, 84 for males and 24 for females.

Contracting and corporatisation of prisons

In 1996–97 the private prisons in NSW, Qld, Vic. and SA held a total of 1862 prisoners.

Prisoner numbers

In 1982 the total Australian prisoner population was 9826; by 1995 it had increased to 17 428, while prisoners awaiting trial had grown from 996 in 1982 to 1990 in 1995. In December 1995 the average prison population was 16 059, i.e. 117.5 per 100 000 of adult population.

▶ 95% of prisoners were male. The male rate of daily prisoner population was 227.1 per 100 000 of adult population compared with a female rate of 10.8.

▶ Prisoners are mainly in the younger age groups and the 1995 median age was 31 years.

▶ Across the states and territories in 1994–95 the number of prisoners per uniformed officer ranged from 2.4 in NSW to 1.4 in Tas.

▶ The costs per prisoner per day ranged from $143 in the NT to $104 in SA.

▶ In 1994 42% of prisoners had a minimum security classification, 26% had a medium security classification, 16% had a maximum security classification and 16% were unclassified.

▶ In June 1994 13.4% had been convicted of break and enter, 13.2% of sex offences, 11.5% of drug offences, 10.8% of assault and 9% of homicide.

▸ Of a total of 16 944 prisoners in June 1994, 14 998 had been sentenced and 1946 were on remand.

▸ Violent assaults and sexual offences accounted for about 47% of the offences for which people were in gaol as at June 1996, while property offences accounted for about 28%. For males the most common offences were sexual offences, break and enter, robbery and assault. For females the most common offences were fraud and misappropriation, dealing and trafficking in drugs, and break and enter.

Juvenile corrective institutions

As at June 1993 there were 610 males and 41 females aged 10–17 years in juvenile corrective institutions compared with 1119 males and 233 females as at June 1981.

Australians in foreign prisons

According to the Department of Foreign Affairs and Trade there were 175 Australians in foreign gaols in 1996, 86 were on remand and 89 had

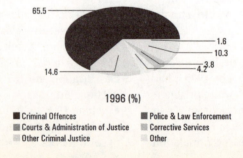

Estimated Cost of Crime and Justice

1996 (%)

- Criminal Offences
- Courts & Administration of Justice
- Other Criminal Justice
- Police & Law Enforcement
- Corrective Services
- Other

been sentenced. Twenty were imprisoned in Thailand, 19 in NZ, 17 in the USA and 15 in Greece.

Costs of maintaining public prisons
Maintaining public prisons in Australia in 1994–95 entailed a recurrent expenditure of more than $814m.

Prison escapes
The total prison escape rate per 100 prisoner years in 1996–97 ranged from zero in the ACT to 4 in WA.

◗ The escape rate from secure custody ranged from zero in the NT to 0.3 per 100 prisoners in NSW.

◗ The escape rate from open custody ranged from 2.4 in Vic. to 11.5 in WA.

Deaths from apparent unnatural causes
In 1996–97 deaths from apparent unnatural causes per 100 prisoner years ranged from zero in Tas. and the NT to 0.4 (nine deaths) in WA.

Government current expenditure on public order and safety
In 1994–95 all Australian governments spent $5755m on current outlays and $496m on capital outlays in connection with public order and safety.

ENTERTAINMENT AND RECREATION

Recreation
Recreation is the relaxation and enjoyment afforded by a pastime, exercise, diversion or other pursuit.

National parks
During 1995–96 there were 3.48 million visitors to national parks, 2.61 million being born in Australia and 870 000 born overseas.

◗ 950 000 of these visitors were aged 25–34 years and 940 000 35–44 years, 590 000 45–54 years and 450 000 18–24 years.

Recreational fishing
A 1984 survey found that one-third of

the population aged over 10 went fishing at least once a year. In the year ended April 1992 people fishing for recreation and leisure had an estimated catch of 23 152 t of fish, 2800 t of crabs and 1400 t of yabbies/marron.

- On average every Australian household setting a net or casting a line caught 27.1 kg of seafood.
- Qld anglers landed almost 7300 t of seafood, NSW 5200 t and WA 5200 t.

Household expenditure on recreation

In 1993–94 the average household spent $76.38 per week on recreation.

Cultural activities
Cultural venues

In the 12 months to 31 March 1995 11.7 million people (about 83% of the Australian population) aged 15 years and over had been to at least one of the cultural venues and activities that were surveyed. The highest cultural centre attended was the cinema, which was visited by 8.7 million persons (62.1% of the population).

- Residents of the ACT had the highest participation rate of all states and territories for the 12 selected venues and activities.
- Females reported a higher participation rate than males.
- The participation rate was 38.5% at botanical gardens, 38.4% at libraries and 35.3% at animal and marine parks.
- 7.7% had attended classical music concerts.

Museums and art museums

Museums Australia surveyed 283 larger museums with paid staff in 1995. The results showed that total operating expenditure was $351m and total income was $341.9m.

- 3.9 million people attended museums and 3.14 million art museums in 1994–95.
- Volunteers contributed 23 900 hours, an increase of 44% from the previous year.
- Australians' interest in major

museums is illustrated in the attendance and other statistics of the Australian National Maritime Museum.

- 395 928 visitors attended the museum in 1995–96, up 28% on 1994–95.
- Parties from 935 schools with 40 716 students visited the museum.
- There were 56 194 guided tours with 89 640 participants.
- Visitor entry revenue was $1.43m, augmented by $108 615 in merchandising and other revenues.

Botanical gardens

The Australian National Botanic Gardens in Canberra maintain 85 000 plants, representing approximately one-third of the vascular plants recorded for Australia. There are also significant botanical gardens in all the state capitals, especially in Sydney and Melbourne.

▶ In 1994–95 5.41 million people aged 15 and over visited botanical gardens.

Zoological and marine parks

The first zoo in Australia was founded in Melbourne in 1857. There are now 42 Australian institutional members of the Regional Association of Zoological Parks and Aquaria. Taronga Zoo, a major attraction in Sydney, also maintains the Western Plains Zoo at Dubbo, which has an internationally recognised program for threatened species from throughout the world.

▶ 4.9 million, or 35.3% of the population aged 15 years and over, attended animal and marine parks during 1994–95.

Libraries and book usage

The National Library, state and public libraries had a book stock of 29.5 million in 1994–95 compared with 26.8 million in 1989–90.

▶ The 1995 attendance at libraries reached 5.4 million. 5329 million books were bought or borrowed in 1994.

Reading habits

In February 1995 a household survey found that 87.9% of males and 82.4% of females aged 18 years and over had read a newspaper, and 46.8% of males and 57.8% of females had read a book in the week preceding the survey.

▌ Australians spent an average of $61 on books in 1993–94, with the ACT the highest at $96 per person and Tas. the lowest at $54 per person.

Book publishing

In 1994 186 organisations engaged in book publishing had a turnover of $1156.7m, $841.7m coming from the sale of books.

▌ $487.7m of those sales were attributed to Australian titles.

Music, dancing and the performing arts

The Australian Ballet

The Australian Ballet, the nation's classical ballet company, was founded in 1961. In 1995 it had 146 employees of whom 65 were dancers. It presented 175 performances in 1995, in eight venues throughout the country.

Musica Viva

Founded in 1945 as a non-profit company, Musica Viva is the national chamber music entrepreneur. In 1995 it presented concerts to audiences of 379 740 in Australia and 52 000 overseas.

ABC Symphony Orchestras

Until 1997 the Australian Broadcasting Corporation, through ABC Concerts, controlled six state symphony orchestras; in that year the orchestras were established as separate entities with their own funding. In 1995–96 the orchestras gave 496 paid orchestral concerts, 144 school concerts and 15 free concerts, with a total of 987 433 people attending.

▌ In February 1997 it was reported that 21.9% of persons aged 18 years and over, 30.9% of those aged 18–24 and 9.7% of those aged 65 years and over had attended arts festivals in the last 12 months.

Cultural occupations

In 1994 of the students wishing to be artists who entered tertiary institutions 25.1% enrolled in Fine Arts courses, 20.9% in Music, 17.9% in the Visual and Graphic Arts and 4.8% in the Dramatic Arts. At the time of the 1991 census there were 17 293 designers and illustrators, 6989 musicians and composers, 5712 visual artists and 5245 photographers in Australia.

▶ A survey of artists in 1993 showed that the median income of composers was $21 700, community artists $15 400, musicians (including singers) $14 500, craftspeople $11 000 and dancers and choreographers $8300.

Cultural funding

A total of $3195.0m was provided by governments for cultural funding in 1995–96, an increase of 4.7% on 1994–95. The Commonwealth government provided 42.9%, state/territory governments 38.1% and local government 18.9%.

▶ Cultural facilities and services received the largest share at $1346.3m (42.1%), with libraries and archives at $588.9m being the main recipients.

▶ Broadcasting and film received $914.2m and recreational facilities and services $774.5m.

▶ $805m for radio and television broadcasting was the largest item of the funding for broadcasting and film.

▶ In 1995–96 all Australian governments combined spent $42.40 per head of population on recreational facilities and services, $74.00 per head on cultural facilities and services, and $50.30 per head on broadcasting and film.

▶ The Commonwealth government's contribution for cultural funding in

1995–96 was $75.40 per head, state/territory governments share was $66.90 per head and local government's share was $33.30 per head. The total contribution for all levels of government was $175.60 per head.

◗ At $2756.1m, most cultural funding was of a recurrent nature. Capital funds allocated were $438.9m, of which the states and territories contributed $215.9m and local government $136.9m.

The film and video production industry

The year 1995 marked 100 years of film production in Australia. In 1994 there were 1179 businesses in the film and video production industry, employing 5998 persons and generating $467.7m from sales and services, and $121.2m from the sales of rights for completed works.

◗ During 1993–94 the industry spent $463m on the production of films and videos, $184.2m on productions for television, $143.4m on productions other than for television (including $87.3m on feature films) and $135.4m on the production of commercials and advertisements.

◗ 29 feature films were in production or were made during 1993–94.

◗ 998 people were employed in the industry. NSW accounted for 58% of the industry's employment and 59% of the gross income. Vic. was responsible for 28% of employment.

◗ Small businesses with less than 20 employees accounted for 96% of all business in the industry.

Motion picture exhibition industry

In recent years the Australian cinema industry has been characterised by the development of multi-screen cinema complexes, which also provide other attractions, e.g. computerised games and associated food outlets. There were 701 cinemas in 1985; in 1993–94 there were 224 cinemas, employing 5729 people.

▶ In 1995 1.14 million Australians had gone to a cinema once only, whereas 257 200 had attended more than 30 times. There has been a marked increase in the number of multi-screen cinemas. As at June 1997 there were 565 theatres with 1309 screens.

▶ In 1996 national box office takings were $536.77m and estimated attendances were 73.95 million. Paid admissions totalled 61.1 million.

▶ 278 films were released in 1996, of which 24 were Australian, 184 American and 26 were from the UK.

▶ The top films in 1996 in box-office takings were *Independence Day* ($29.29m), *Babe* ($25.8m) and *Twister* ($23.44m).

Video hiring and watching

In 1996 about 700 million videos were hired. The top videos in terms of hirings were *While You Were Sleeping*, *Seven* and *Jumanji*.

▶ The top-selling video in 1996 was *Toy Story*.

▶ A survey in 1994 found that almost 60% of households with children had watched a video in the previous week.

▶ 39.5 % of adults had watched a video in the same period.

▶ 79.3% of all homes had a video recorder and almost 58% had hired a video in the prior month.

Sport
Participation in sport

In the 12 months ended June 1996 4 224 200 (30.7%) people aged 15 years and over participated in organised sport and physical activities.

▶ The male participation rate was 34% compared with a female rate of 27.4%.

▶ The 15–19 age group had the highest participation rate, 61.4% for males and 50.1% for females.

▶ For people aged 65 years and over only 17.7% participated in organised sport and physical activities.

◗ The NT with 38.6% had the highest participation rate among the states/territories and NSW the lowest at 28.7%.

Government expenditure on sport

The total expenditure on sport at the Commonwealth, state/territory and local government level was $1661m in 1994–5 compared with $1579m in 1993–94. The Commonwealth government provided $20m under the Olympic Athlete Program to assist in the preparation of athletes for the 2000 Sydney Olympic and Paralympic Games.

◗ During 1996 funding was provided by the Australian Sports Commission to 114 organisations; 16 national organisations each received over $1m.

Personal expenditures on sport

During 1995–96 participants spent $2755m on sport and physical activities, the main expenses being transport and weekly fees ($986.3m), clothing and equipment ($906.7m), membership ($549.6m) and other expenses ($312.6m).

◗ Participants spent an average of $652 in 1995–96 on sport and physical activities.

Five most popular organised sports and physical activities

For persons aged 15 years and over 669 900 persons took part in aerobics in 1995–96, 444 700 in golf, 363 000 in tennis, 328 600 in netball and 296 400 in lawn bowls.

Three most expensive organised sports and physical activities

Horse riding, at an annual average cost per person of $1833, was the most expensive sport in 1995–96, followed by motor sports at $1653 and air sports at $1301.

Children's participation in sport

Of all children aged 5–14 years in 1995–96, 61.5% took part in at least one organised sport or physical activity, ranging from 74.6% in the ACT to 54.9% in Vic.

▶ Swimming (338 800) and basketball (300 100) were the most popular organised activities.

▶ 21.6% of children took part in activities organised by schools in after-school hours, ranging from a high of 36.1% in SA to 18.8% in NSW.

▶ 53.5% of children took part in sport or physical activities organised by clubs, ranging from a high of 64% in the ACT to 41.1% in Tas.

Sports injuries

A survey was conducted in 1996 with 25 525 NSW respondents aged 11–19 years, of whom 92% indicated they had participated in at least one sport in the previous 12 months.

▶ 30% had participated in basketball, 24% in soccer, 23% in swimming, 20% in tennis, 15% in netball, 15% in cricket and 13% in rugby league.

▶ 54% of those who had participated in sport received at least one injury in the previous six months.

▶ Males sustained slightly more injuries than females (1.12 males:1 females).

▶ 36% of participants in rugby union, 35% in rugby league, 34% in gymnastics, 33% in netball and 31% in Australian Rules football suffered injuries.

▶ The most common sites for injuries were ankle (32%), knee (30%), finger (15%), upper leg (12%) and lower leg (11%). In some cases a respondent reported injuries in more than one site.

Sports attendance

An ABS survey in March 1995 found that 6.2 million people aged 15 years and over went at least once to a sporting event in the last 12 months. There were 3.5 million males compared to 2.7 million females.

▶ 1 874 200 people saw at least one Australian Rules football game and of these 553 300 had attended 10 games or more.

▶ Horse racing (1.7 million), rugby league (1.5 million) and cricket (1.2 million) follow Australian Rules as the sports most attended at least once.

▶ The record sporting attendance was 121 696 at the Australian Rules football match at the Melbourne Cricket Ground for the 1970 Grand Final of Carlton v. Collingwood.

Sports industries operations

There were 5090 sports industries businesses in 1994–95, with 906 in horse and dog racing, 1566 sports grounds and facilities, and 2618 sports and services to sport.

Employment and volunteers in sports industries

At 30 June 1995 there were 37 689 males and 24 682 females employed in the sports industries, including horse and dog racing. There were also 113 825 volunteers involved in operations of the sports industries.

Sports industries financial operations

There was a total income of $2678.7m in 1994–95, including $757m from admissions, subscriptions, membership and playing fees, $312.1m from sponsors, advertising, and television/radio rights, $217.4 from catering. Expenses totalled $2517.8m, of which labour costs at $685.1m was the largest item.

Gambling

In Australia there are many forms of licensed gambling: horse racing, greyhound racing, bingo, lotteries, pools, poker machines and keno. Illegal gambling is also common. There are licensed casinos in every state and territory and on Christmas Island. The states and territories obtain many millions of dollars annually from taxation on gambling turnover. In 1994–95 there were 2041 businesses in the gambling services industry employing 32 062 persons at 30 June 1995. The industry had a total income of $15 511m, which after expenses, including taxes, levies and other government charges, resulted in an operating profit before tax of $1292.2m.

Horse and dog racing

Match racing of horses had begun in Sydney by the 1790s and the first race meeting was held at Parramatta (NSW) on 30 April 1810. Today much on-course betting at racecourses is conducted on the automatic totalisator invented by George Julius in 1916. Betting with licensed bookmakers is also permitted. Off-course betting may also be carried out at Totalisator Agency Boards (TABs) which have been set up throughout the country. Betting on a wide range of sporting and other events can now be carried out by licensed bookmakers and TABs. There were 898 horse and dog racing businesses at 30 June 1995, employing 14 118 staff and having an operating profit before tax of $793.2m.

Per capita expenditure on gambling

	current prices ($)
1972–73	52.40
1977–78	113.16
1982–83	177.21
1987–88	281.18
1992–93	453.03
1993–94	527.12

The Melbourne Cup

First run in Melbourne in 1861 and traditionally contested on the first Tuesday in November, the race is regarded as one of the nation's premier sporting events and large sums are wagered on the result.

▶ Carbine in 1890 carried the greatest weight (66 kg) to win.
▶ Phar Lap in 1930 was the race's winner at the shortest betting price (11/8 on).
▶ The Pearl (1871), Wotan (1936) and Old Rowley (1940) won at 100 to 1.

Lotteries

As at 30 June 1995 there were 178 licensed lotteries, employing 2006 people, with a gross income of $4134.4m.

Poker machines

Illegal poker machines (one-armed bandits) were in use in Australia from the 1900s. NSW permitted registered clubs to operate poker machines in 1956; their use is now widespread and they have been incorporated in hotels and casinos.

Casinos

At 30 June 1996 there were 14 casinos operating in Australia; they employed staff of 15 837 and had an operating profit before tax of $198m.

State and territory taxes on gambling

In 1990–91 state taxes on gambling totalled $1646m, of which casino taxes were $93m. The 1995–96 taxes collected on gambling were $3306m, of which $367m came from casino taxes. Poker-machine taxes were $1256m in 1995–96 compared with $295m in 1990–91. In the same period race betting taxes remained static at about $650m.

Takings by Type of Gambling
1995–96

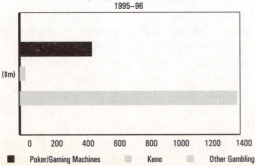

■ Poker/Gaming Machines   Keno   Other Gambling

STRUCTURE OF GOVERNMENT

The six founding states of Australia were federated in 1901 by the formation of the Commonwealth of Australia. There are now three levels of government operating throughout the country: federal, state and local. Areas of power not specified in Section 51 of the Constitution are the responsibility of the states and territories. The legislative power of the Commonwealth is vested in the Parliament, which consists of the Queen, the Senate (Upper House) and the House of Representatives (Lower House). The Queen is represented by the Governor-General. Each state and territory has its own parliament and in the case of the states, a state Governor is the Queen's representative. In 1996 there were 842 elected members of Parliament, 224 being Commonwealth members and 618 state and territory members.

- The first Parliament of the Commonwealth of Australia opened on 9 May 1901.
- All state parliaments are bicameral, except for Qld, which abolished its Upper House in 1922.
- There have been 39 Governors-General. His Excellency the Honourable Sir William Deane is the present holder of the office.
- Sir Isaac Isaacs was the first Australian-born Governor-General (1931–36).

Voting
The franchise

Any Australian citizen aged 18 years or over is qualified to become an elector. Enrolment and voting are compulsory for all eligible voters.

- At the 1996 general election the national enrolment was 11 740 568 voters. There were 228 eligible voters stationed in Antarctica.
- SA introduced universal adult suffrage in 1896 when it extended

the franchise to women. The Commonwealth followed suit in 1902 and by 1908 all other states had done likewise.

▶ In August 1943 Dame Dorothy Tangey was the first woman elected to the Senate, as a member of the Australian Labor Party (ALP) from WA.

▶ Neville Bonner was the first Aboriginal member of the Commonwealth Parliament, when he was elected to the Senate in 1972 as a member of the Liberal Party from Qld.

▶ After the 1996 general election 148 members had been elected to the House of Representatives and 76 to the Senate.

▶ After the 1996 general election there were 23 women sitting in the House of Representatives and 23 in the Senate: this was the highest-ever representation by women.

Voting systems

Voting at elections is by way of a proportional preferential system.

▶ In the 1996 general election, 3.2% of the votes were informal.

▶ Secret ballots, which are used in elections at all levels of government, were introduced in Qld and Vic. in 1856.

Compulsory voting

Qld adopted the principle of compulsory voting in 1915, which has since been extended to all three levels of government throughout Australia.

▶ A 1996 Herald AGB/McNair opinion poll found that 72% of respondents were in favour of compulsory voting.

▶ An Australian National University survey of candidates at the 1996 general election found that 96.3% of Australian Labor Party, 82% of Australian Democrat, 80.6% of Greens and 40.4% of Liberal/National Party candidates favoured compulsory voting.

Commonwealth government
The Senate

The Senate is presently made up of

76 members, 12 elected by each of the states, and two each for the ACT and NT. No government has had a majority in the Senate since 1981, and the ruling party often has to rely on the support of minor parties or independents in order to have legislation enacted. Senators are elected for a term of six years. An election for half the members of the Senate is held at each general election, unless there has been a double dissolution of Parliament, in which case a full Senate election is held.

The House of Representatives

According to the Constitution, the number of members in the Lower House must be as near as is practicable twice that of the Senate. The number of electorates is presently set at 148. Members are elected for the duration of the Parliament, which is limited to three years.

Referendums

Any proposed law to alter the Constitution must be passed by a majority in both houses, must be submitted to a referendum in each state and territory, and must by approved by a majority of voters in a majority of states and by a majority of all voters. Since 1901, 42 proposals have gone to referendums and the consent of electors has been obtained in eight instances, probably the most significant being that relating to the constitutional rights of Aboriginal people in 1967.

◗ Several referendum questions were submitted to electors on 3 September 1988, using 10 777 polling places at a total cost of $34.25m. None of the proposals were approved.

◗ In addition to referendums for alterations to the Constitution, other Commonwealth referendums have been put to the nation: two before Federation in connection with the proposed Constitution, and two in respect to military service during the First World War. On 21 May 1977, a national song poll was conducted, with preferential voting, and as a result 'Advance Australia Fair' was adopted as Australia's national song.

Election funding for political parties

To be eligible for election funding provided by the government, a candidate or Senate group must win at least 4% of the formal first-preference vote in the division or state contested. In the 1996 general election the various parties received $13.16m in election funding.

Commonwealth Parliamentary elections – 2 March 1996

▶ There were 11 740 568 voters enrolled and 11 244 017 votes recorded, with 360 165 informal votes.

▶ The Australian Labor Party gained 4 217 765 first-preference votes in the election for the House of Representatives, the Liberal Party gained 4 210 689, the National Party 893 170, the Australian Democrats 735 848, the Greens 317 654, and all other groups 150 008.

▶ After the half-election for the Senate there were 29 Australian Labor Party, 31 Liberal Party, seven Australian Democrat, six National Party of Australia and two Greens senators, and one independent. Senator Mal Colston (Qld), who had been elected as a

State of the parties, Federal Parliament – September 1996

House of Representatives		Senate	
Australian Labor Party	49	Australian Labor Party	28
Liberal Party	76	Liberal Party	31
National Party of Australia	18	National Party of Australia	6
Independent	5	Australian Democrats	7
		the Greens	2
		Independent	2

candidate for the Australian Labor Party, later left the party and became an independent. Together with Senator Brian Harradine (Tas.), he held the balance of power in the Senate.

State government

All state parliaments have Upper and Lower Houses except Qld, which abolished its Upper House in 1922. NT and ACT have only one house. The leader of the government party in state governments is known as the Premier. A Governor is appointed by the Queen on advice from the premier of the state. He or she assents to bills passed by the state and has the prerogative of mercy.

◗ Dr Carmen Lawrence in 1989 in WA and Mrs Joan Kirner in 1990 in Vic. were the first women to become premiers of state governments.

◗ There have been 36 governors of NSW since Captain Arthur Phillip (1788–90). Aboriginal pastor Sir Douglas Nicholls became Governor of SA on 1 December 1976 and was the first Aboriginal person appointed to the office.

◗ Dame Roma Mitchell was the first woman to become a state governor when she was appointed Governor of SA in 1990.

Local government

Local councils are elected by adult franchise from registered electors. The states require these councils to be responsible for a range of functions – which may vary from area to area – including the maintenance of roads and bridges, drainage and sanitation, the supervision of housing and the provision of recreational facilities. In June 1996 there were 754 local councils with a total annual expenditure of about $15 166m. They received Commonwealth and state/territory grants of $9767m. They also raised $5428m by way of taxes and fees.

◗ About 60% of councils are rural,

and many are small, with less than 5000 electors.
- There is a trend for councils to amalgamate and a growing number have populations of 100 000 or more, e.g. City of Brisbane (780 000), City of the Gold Coast (300 000), City of Blacktown (225 000).
- In 1996, there were 12 Aboriginal people elected to councils in NSW, 14 in WA, two in SA and eight in Qld. In the NT there are about 400 Aboriginal people who are elected members of Community Government Councils.

Taxation

In 1800 Governor Hunter instituted the first taxes in the colony of NSW, when import duties were imposed on spirits, wine and beer. The revenue was to be used to build a gaol. The states collected their own income taxes until 1942, when the Commonwealth government assumed that responsibility. The states are now reimbursed according to a formula (which is amended from time to time) applied by the Commonwealth Grants Commission.

The Commonwealth government has exclusive responsibility under the provisions of the Constitution for a wide range of functions, including defence, foreign affairs, trade and immigration. It levies and collects all income tax from individuals as well as from enterprises, and also collects other taxes such as those on goods and services. Part of this tax revenue is distributed by the central government to other levels of government, mainly to the states and territories.
- The taxation collection by all levels of government in 1996–97 amounted to $8813 per head of population, an increase of 7.3% over the $8214 of 1995–96. The Commonwealth government share was $6740 per head and the average share of the states and territories was $2073.
- As a percentage of GDP total taxation revenue rose from 30.7% in

1995–96 to 32% in 1996–97. Commonwealth government taxation revenue increased from 23.7% to 24.5% and state, territory and local government revenue from 7.3% to 7.5%.

- There was an increase in the contribution to total taxes in all categories ranging from 40.7% taxes on incomes, 133.3% taxes levied on enterprises, 1.8% for fines and fees.

Commonwealth government taxes, fees and fines accounted for 76.5% of taxation revenue from all governments. The Commonwealth government collected $124 638m in taxes, fees and fines in 1996–97, a rise of 7.9% on the $115 486m collected in 1995–96. There was growth in all major tax categories apart from some specific taxes, e.g. taxes on agricultural production and levies on statutory authorities.

- It cost the Commonwealth government $1104.9m to collect a total of $98 373m in 1995–96.

- State, territory and local government taxation totalled $38 323m in 1996–97, an increase of 7% on the previous year. The ACT, at 11.5%, had the highest growth in taxation revenue, followed by the NT at 10.4% and NSW at 8.7%. Tas. and WA had the lowest levels of increase at 2.2% and 3.9% respectively.

- Local government collected $5705m in taxes on property and fees and fines in 1996–97, compared with $5511m the previous year.

Total taxation revenue, 1995

	(% of GDP)
Denmark	51.3
Sweden	49.7
France	44.5
Greece	41.4
Italy	41.3
New Zealand	38.2
Canada	37.2
United Kingdom	35.3
Australia	**30.7**
Japan	28.5
United States	27.9

Personal income tax
Income taxes levied on individuals were $66 278m in 1996–97 compared with $60 602m in 1995–96, an increase of 9.36%.

Income tax levied on enterprises
A total of $21 706m in income tax was levied on enterprises in 1996–97, an increase of 12.5% on the $19 287m of the previous year.

Income tax levied on non-residents
Total income taxes levied on non-residents were $1238m in 1996–97, of which $519m was Interest Withholding Tax and $556m was Dividend Withholding Tax.

Sales tax and excises
In 1996–97 sales taxes levied by the Commonwealth government were $13 293m compared with $12 970m in 1995–96, and excises, fees and levies rose from $13 215m to $14 002m over the same period.

Fringe Benefits Tax (FBT)
In 1991–92 the Commonwealth government collected $1207m from the Fringe Benefits Tax. By 1995–96 it had risen to $2938m, the rise being largely attributable to the use by corporations of salary packages, and to effective administration by the Australian Taxation Office.

Capital Gains Tax (CGT)
In 1995–96, 152 505 taxpayers paid $339m tax on capital gains of $978m.

Refunds of taxation revenue
In 1995–96 there was $9909m in refunds of taxation revenue, a rise of 7.4% on the previous year.

PAYE tax system
About one worker in 10 has dropped out of the pay-as-you-earn system, costing an estimated A$5bn a year in lost taxation revenue. Over 500 000 have left the PAYE system in six years, mainly switching to contract work through family companies or trusts.

Tax evasion

In 1995–96 Australian Taxation Office audits disclosed that companies which had evaded $24m in tax had penalties imposed amounting to $5m, trusts which had evaded $4m were penalised $1m, partnerships which had evaded $2m were penalised $1m, and individuals who had evaded $52m were penalised $18m.

Prosecutions

In 1995–96 the Australian Taxation Office referred 177 audit cases to the Director of Public Prosecutions. There were 1122 convictions and total fines and orders amounted to $3 443 587. In addition, there were 9045 in-house prosecutions resulting in 24 895 convictions and $11 444 296 in penalties and fines.

▶ Twenty-one gaol terms were imposed. There were 32 cases where the verdict was a suspended gaol term or a good behaviour bond, and 755 hours of community service was required of other offenders.

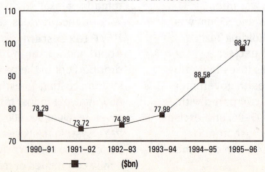

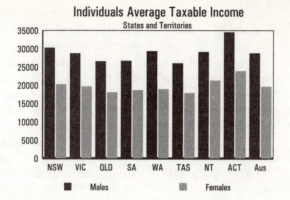

Additional tax for late lodgement of returns

In 1995–96 additional tax of $77 568 107 for late returns was imposed on individuals, $14 734 163 on companies and $2 920 179 on superannuation funds. Remittances totalled $32 510 689.

State/territory finance

The state and territory governments carry out the entire range of activities, other than those which are deemed by the Constitution to be the exclusive domain of the Commonwealth. Their main functions include public order, health, education, administration, transport and the maintenance of infrastructure. The state/territory revenue base is more restricted than the Commonwealth and comprises taxes on property, employers' payrolls and the provision of goods and services. Grants from the Commonwealth supplement this revenue base.

▶ State and territory revenues from

taxes and fees totalled $30 360m in 1995–96, an increase of 7.4% on the previous year.

▶ The states and territories received a total of $34 702m in Commonwealth grants: $27 715m for their own use, and $6987m for passing on to local government and other state/territory authorities.

▶ The states and territories had a total revenue of $74 423m and a total outlay of $64 063m.

▶ Financing and deficit measures were –$10 360m, leading to a deficit adjusted for net advances of –$2820m.

Local government finance

Local government authorities govern areas such as cities, towns, shires, boroughs, municipalities and district councils. Their functions vary according to the state or territory within which they are situated, but in general they are responsible for roads, water, sewerage, drainage systems, health and sanitary services and the supervision of building, as well as various community undertakings. Their main source of revenue is derived from taxes on property, known as rates; they also receive various grants from their own state or territory government and from the Commonwealth government.

▶ In 1995–96 local governments had a total revenue of $15 953m and total outlays of $15 166m. Financing and deficit measures were –$787m, leading to a deficit adjusted for net advances of –$319m.

Consolidated outlays by all governments

In the 1995–96 financial year the Commonwealth, state/territory and local governments disbursed $174 213m, compared with $176 937m in 1994–95. Social security and welfare was the biggest outlay at $49 245m, then came health at $27 424m and education at $23 922m.

Notes and decimal coinage on issue

On the last Wednesday in June 1996 there were notes on issue worth $191 982m and coins worth $1394m. Two-cent coins worth $22.8m and one-cent coins worth $30.7m, which are no longer legal tender, were still in circulation.

▶ For business transactions over the counter, items charged at up to four cents are rounded down to the ten cent below and those charged between five and nine cents are rounded up to the ten cent above.

DEFENCE

A battery of two guns was erected in Sydney Cove in 1788. The last British troops left Australia on 23 August 1870, and the colonies became responsible for their own defences. When the six colonies federated in 1901, the Commonwealth of Australia assumed all responsibility for defence.

Australia in wars

The Maori Wars (1860–65)
When volunteers were recruited in NSW, Vic. and Tas., 2675 men and about 1000 women and children went to New Zealand.

Sudan Campaign (1885)
A NSW volunteer contingent of 522 infantry and 212 artillerymen assisted British forces fighting against the Mahdi's followers. Three men were wounded and six died from fever.

The Boer War (1899–1902)
A total of 16 175 men went to South Africa to assist the British fighting against the Boers. There were 1400 casualties, including 518 killed. Lieutenants Harry (Breaker) Morant and Peter Handcock were executed by the British authorities for war crimes.

The Boxer Rebellion (1899)
In China the Boxers, an anti-foreign and anti-Christian sect, attacked foreign establishments and legations in Beijing and massacred Christian

Chinese. Four hundred Australian naval volunteers were sent to assist the British expeditionary force.

The First World War (1914–18)

All Australians who fought in the First World War were volunteers; they fought on land, at sea and in the air. Referendum proposals in 1915 and 1917 to bring about conscription were defeated.

- 331 000 men and women were enlisted for active service, of whom 59 330 lost their lives and 151 171 were wounded.
- At the outbreak of hostilities Australian forces occupied German New Guinea, which after the war became a League of Nations–mandated territory administered by Australia.
- Together with New Zealand troops, Australians took part in the landing at Anzac Cove, Gallipoli, on 25 April 1915.

The Second World War (1939–45)

Australians again fought on land, at sea and in the air, either in Australian units or in the Royal Air Force or Royal Navy. Australian forces fought against the Germans and Italians in Greece, Crete and Libya. After the attack on Pearl Harbor, Australian forces fought against the Japanese. Twenty thousand Australians became prisoners of war with the fall of Singapore. During the war there was a total enlistment of 926 000 men and 63 100 women.

- 33 552 men and women were killed or died as prisoners of war.
- More than 30 800 Australians became prisoners of war.
- Darwin was the first part of mainland Australia to suffer at the hands of an enemy. The city was bombed by the Japanese on 19 February 1942.
- Three Japanese midget submarines attacked Sydney Harbour on 31 May 1942, sinking the barracks ship *Kattabul* and killing 19 sailors.

▸ Japanese prisoners of war staged an unsuccessful breakout at Cowra, NSW, on 5 August 1944. During the incident 234 Japanese were killed and 108 were wounded; four Australian soldiers died and three were wounded.

The Malayan Emergency (1950–62)

Australian forces assisted the British in counter-insurgency measures in Malaya. A permanent RAAF base was established at Butterworth, and ground troops of the Royal Australian Regiment served in the area up to 1960.

▸ During the period eight Australian military personnel were killed and five were wounded.

The Korean War (1950–53)

The three branches of the Australian Defence Force were part of the United Nations force fighting against the North Koreans and Chinese.

▸ During the war, 339 Australians were killed and 1216 were wounded.

The Vietnam War (1966–72)

All three elements of Australia's armed forces joined with 15 other nations to support the Americans in their campaign against the North Vietnamese and Viet Cong.

▸ The number of Australians who served in Vietnam was 40 207. Of these, 501 were killed and 2398 were injured.

The Persian Gulf War (1991)

Australia participated in the United Nations–sanctioned enforcement operations against Iraq, which had invaded Kuwait. The principal contribution was of frigate support vessels as part of the multi-nation naval force patrolling the Persian Gulf. A mine-clearance team and an Australian Defence Force medical team were also involved in the operation.

Defence force expenditure

Although the government in its 1996 and 1997 budgets reduced overall expenditure, the appropriation for the Australian Defence Force (ADF) was quarantined from any reduction. In 1995–96 the total actual expenditure by the ADF was $999m, with the 1997–98 budget estimate being $10 405m.

Defence service and civilian personnel as at 30 June 1997

Navy
There were 14 701 personnel in the Navy, 84.7% being males and 15.3% females. Officers comprised 17.4%. Females are included in the crews of sea-going ships.

Army
There were 25 885 personnel in the Army, 89.3% being males and 10.7% females. Officers comprised 14.8%. Females are allocated to non-combat functions.

Air Force
There were 14 425 personnel in the Air Force, 83.8% being males and 16.2% females. Officers comprised 19%. Females are included in the crews of non-combatant aircraft.

Civilians
Males made up 67.6% of the 13 537 civilians employed by the defence organisation, and females 32.4%, for a total civilian staff of 13 894. There were 95 male and nine female Senior Executive staff.

Aboriginal people in the defence force
The number of personnel identifying themselves as Aboriginal or Torres Strait Islander increased from 184 in 1994–95 to 204 in 1995–96.

Major military equipment
The Royal Australian Navy fleet
In 1997 the principal vessels in the fleet consisted of three guided missile destroyers, six guided missile frigates, three destroyer escorts, six submarines and 15 patrol boats. The fleet air arm operated 34 helicopters.

The Royal Australian Air Force aircraft

The front-line aircraft in 1997 were F-111 fighter/bombers and F/A-18 tactical fighters.

Office of War Graves

The Commonwealth spent $1.05m in 1996–97 on the establishment, care and maintenance of graves, and computerised the records of Australians who were killed or died in active service.

War veterans

In 1997, 20% of the total war veteran population was aged over 80 years. The 1997 Mortality Study of Vietnam War Veterans concluded that there was an increase of about 7% in the mortality of these veterans compared to the general population. There was an increase in the rate of death from cancers of the head and neck, e.g. throat cancer.

Overseas aid program

It was estimated that on 11 July 1990 (World Population Day), the world's population was 5 594 657 136 and that it was growing at the rate of three people every second, 175 per minute and a quarter of a million every day. Most of the population growth is in developing countries. The United Nations Population Fund predicts that during the next century the world's population could double to over 10 billion, or nearly treble to 14 billion before it stabilises. The developing world has 75% of the world's population but consumes only 15% of the world's energy. A child growing up in the Western world consumes 20 to 40 times more of the world's resources than a child in the Third World.

▶ Australia's development cooperation program aims to help developing countries reduce poverty and raise the standard of living through sustainable development. A major purpose of the program is to assist in the achievement of a secure and equitable international community.

▶ For 1996–97 Australia's official development assistance (ODA) totalled about $1450.1m, a decrease of 10% on 1995–96. This is an ODA to GNP of 0.29%, putting Australia above the current average donation of 0.27% of GNP by members of the Development Assistance Committee of the OECD.

▶ The aid program, which is administered by the Australian Agency for International Development (AusAID), is divided into three main areas: Country and Regional Assistance, Multilateral Assistance and Humanitarian Assistance.

▶ During 1996–97 Australian government bilateral aid flowed to 108 countries, including $319.5m to

Australian official development assistance, current prices, in $m

1971–72	1976–77	1981–82	1986–87	1991–92	1996–97
200.5	386.2	657.8	975.6	1386	1450.1

Official development assistance by international donors, 1994

	% of donor nations' GNP	Per capita US$
Australia	0.35	61
Canada	0.43	77
France	0.64	146
Germany	0.34	84
Japan	0.29	106
New Zealand	0.24	31
Sweden	0.96	209
United Kingdom	0.31	55
United States	0.15	38

Australian Commonwealth contributions for refugee and emergency relief, in $m

1991–92	1992–93	1993–94	1994–95	1995–96
66	66.4	68.8	70.8	84

Papua New Guinea, $108m to Indonesia, $63.6m to Vietnam, $60m to the Philippines, $41.7m to China and $32.2m to Bangladesh.

▶ In 1996–97 Commonwealth government grants and contributions to United Nations organisations and peacekeeping operations totalled $75.673m, including the United Nations itself $20.27m, UNESCO $7.49m, OECD $7.49m, FAO $6.5m, UN Interim Force in Lebanon $2.54m and the UN Angola Verification Mission $6.35m.

▶ Australian government aid contributions to other international organisations amounted to $380.11m in 1995–96, including $188.56m to multilateral development banks and $10.56m to Commonwealth of Nations organisations.

ECONOMIC OVERVIEW

Inflation
If 1989–90 is taken as the base rate of 100, the 1995–96 inflation rate for all countries was 118.7, a rise of 4.04% on the previous year.

Price indexes
Consumer Price Index (CPI)
The CPI is a measure of inflation or the cost of living. It records against a base figure, in this case 1989–90 = 100, the rise or fall in prices of a range of goods and services. A weighted average is also calculated for the eight capital cities. For the March 1997 quarter the CPI was 120.8. Housing had fallen 2.9% over the previous quarter, health and personal care had risen 2.7%, as had recreation and education 1.9%, food 0.7% and transportation 0.6%.

Consumer Price Indices 1995–96

	(1990=100)
Australia	**115.3**
Canada	112.5
France	112.9
Italy	130.8
Japan	106.2
New Zealand	112.0
United Kingdom	119.6
United States	118.2

Import price index
For March 1997 there was a fall of 5.6% in the import price index, the largest decrease since August 1995, brought about by an increase in the value of the Australian dollar against the major trading countries. Taking 1989–90 as the base year = 100, the 1995–96 import price index was 115.9.

Export price index
During March 1997 the export price index for all groups fell by 1.4%, a principal cause being the appreciation of the dollar against the major trading currencies. Other

significant movements were prices for coal and iron ore falling due to the appreciation of the Australian dollar, and lower world market prices leading to a fall in gold and wheat prices. Taking 1989–90 as the base year = 100 the 1995–96 export price index was 98.8. It fell further to 92.8 in March 1997.

Indexes of industrial production
In 1996 there was a steady growth in the total industrial production index, with a 0.5% increase in the September quarter.

International accounts and trade

Exports of goods and services
Total exports of goods and services for 1995–96, based on an average of 1989–90 prices, was $97 859m, a rise of 9.42% on the previous year.

◗ Total rural exports were worth $20 482m, with wool and sheepskins the biggest single contributor at $4760m, followed by cereal grains and cereal preparations at $3930m and meat and meat preparations at $3620m.

◗ Total non-rural exports were worth $56 994m, with metal ores and minerals the biggest single contributor at $10 499m, followed by machinery at $9252m and coal, coke and briquettes at $7774m.

◗ Coal was the leading single export commodity (10%); non-monetary gold at $5625m and wheat at $3363m were the next two most valuable exports.

◗ Exports of services were valued at $77 476m, a rise of 5.6% on the previous year.

Destinations of merchandise exports
The Asia–Pacific Economic Co-operation (APEC) grouping was Australia's most important regional destination for exports in 1995–96. Japan, at $16 419m, was by far the largest customer, next being the Republic of Korea at $6609m, New

Zealand $5591m, and the USA at $4601m. The European Union (EU) countries took $8454m of Australian exports, the UK being responsible for $2826m, Italy $1281m and Germany $1151m.

Major commodity exports

Of coal exports in 1995–96, Japan took 43% of the exports, the Republic of Korea 13% and India 8%. Non-monetary gold exports brought in $5625m (7% of total exports), with the Republic of Korea buying 39% and Singapore 21%. Wheat at $3363m contributed 4% to total exports and iron ore at $2863m another 4%.

Imports of goods and services

Total imports of goods and services in 1995–96 was $99 653m, a rise of 5.26% on the previous year.

◗ Total consumption goods were valued at $16 886m, of which non-industrial transport equipment (cars etc.), at $2925m, was the biggest single contributor, followed by textiles and clothing at $2638m and food and beverages $2370m.

◗ Total capital goods were worth $21 903m, of which ADP (automatic data processing, i.e. computers) equipment was the single biggest contributor at $8850m, followed by machinery and industrial equipment at $6719m and telecommunications equipment at $2579m. Civil aircraft cost $622m.

Source countries of imports

Total 1995–96 imports from APEC countries were worth $51 942m. The USA was the source of $17 572m, Japan $10 817m and China $4010m of those imports. EU countries provided $19 387m of Australia's imports, $4882m from the UK, $4867m from Germany and $2231m from Italy.

Major commodity imports

Passenger motor vehicles were the most expensive imports in 1995–96 at $3938m, being 5% of total imports. Japan provided 49%, the Republic of

Korea 16%, Germany 13% and the UK 7% of the total cost. Computer equipment comprised 5% of total imports, with the United States contributing 29%, Singapore 20%, Japan 16% and Taiwan 12%. Telecommunications equipment, at 3% of total imports, was the third largest import: the USA provided 21%, Japan 14%, Sweden 13% and Germany 13%. Aircraft and associated equipment made up 3% of total imports: the USA providing 72%, the UK 10%, France 7% and Canada 4%.

Balance of payments

The balance of payments registers the profitability of Australia's trading position in relation to its overseas partners.

◗ For 1996–97 the balance on the current account was –$17 531m, compared with –$21 824m the previous year.

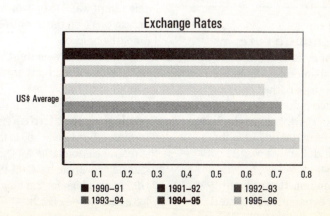

▶ The current account deficit for the March quarter 1998 was $7033m, an increase of 16% on $962m in the December quarter of 1997.

Total merchandise exports and imports

Excess of exports over imports

	$m
1991–92	4043
1992–93	1127
1993–94	78
1994–95	–7567
1995–96	–1878
1996–97	–92

The exchange rate

The exchange rate is the value of the Australian dollar when it is exchanged for another currency. The most commonly quoted rate is against the US dollar. On the last day of trading in April 1996 the Australian dollar was worth $US 0.7854.

▶ The economic downturn in 1998 of the Asian economies impacted severely on the Australian exchange rate and on 6 August 1998 the Australian dollar was worth US$0.6061.

Foreign debt

The net foreign debt is the measure of borrowing by Australian residents at a particular date equated with Australia's total foreign debt. This is calculated by deducting the level of Australian lending abroad and official reserve assets from the level of borrowing. On 30 June 1996 the net foreign debt was $187 804m, an increase of 3% on the $181 972m of 12 months before.

▶ Public-sector foreign debt was $69 130m and that of the private sector $118 674m.

Stock market indexes

If 31 December 1979 = 500 is taken as the reference point, the All Ordinaries index daily average for April 1997 was 2410.2, with a high for the month of 2488 and a low of 2352.2.

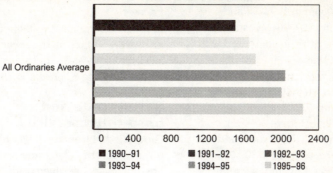

Foreign investment
International investment in Australia

In 1994–95 there was a total of $400 943m foreign investment in Australia, compared with $370 795m in 1993–94 and $266 609m in 1989–90. At 30 June 1995 the USA had the highest level of investment in Australia, at $88 649m, followed by the UK with $76 034m and Japan with $50 913m. Investment income for 1994–95 was $23 710m.

▶ In December 1996 $602.3bn of equity was on issue in Australia, of which the rest of the world held $182bn or 30%. Foreign investors held 44% of the equity in private corporate trading enterprises.

Australian investment abroad

In 1994–95 Australia had $141 226m invested abroad, $35 683m in the USA, followed by the UK at $27 709m and NZ at $10 746m. Total overseas investment by

Australia was $141 226m, compared with $133 060m in 1993–94 and $96 221m in 1989–90. Investment income was $6552m compared with $3961m of 1989–90.

Foreign investment in Australian industries

As at 30 June 1995 the industry group with the highest level of foreign investment was the finance and insurance category at $132 608m (33%), followed by manufacturing at $76 426m and government administration and defence at $74 765m.

Foreign ownership in Australia

At 31 December 1996, of the total equity on issue by Australian corporations $420.3bn (70%) was held by residents and $182.0bn (30%) by non-residents. Non-residents held 44% of private corporate trading enterprises.

◗ 1% of the equity in Australian banks was in foreign ownership.

Company profits before taxes

In 1987–88 company profits before taxes were $14 655m; they reached $25 216m in 1994–95, before falling away by 1.5% to $24 838m in 1995–96.

Retail trade and hospitality/services

Growth in the trend estimate of turnover for the retail trade and hospitality/services increased by 0.2% in May 1998, continuing the weak increase of 0.3% for the previous seven months. In the three months to May 1998 the trend estimate grew by $86.5m, with the only industries to record growth being hospitality and services ($52.2m), food retailing ($27.6m), other retailing ($21.7m) and clothing retailing ($14.6m).

◗ Retail turnover of domestic appliances decreased by 11.9% in May 1998, compared with May 1997. Takeaway food retailing decreased by 8.9% and domestic hardware by 1%.

Small businesses

In February 1995 there were 1.252 million small-business operators, of whom 66.12% were males and 33.88% were females.

▶ 11.6% of the operators were aged less than 30 years, 65.17% were aged 30–50 years and 23.23% were aged over 50 years.

▶ 41.08% of the operators had secondary school qualifications, 33.29% had basic or skilled vocational skills, and 24.80% had a degree or diploma.

▶ 72.24% of the operators were born in Australia and 27.74% were born overseas.

Electronic Funds Transfer (EFT) and credit card transactions

In the year to 31 March 1996 there were 1.14 billion EFT transactions.

▶ At 30 June 1996 there were 116 704 EFTPOS terminals that had handled 470 million transactions in the preceding year.

▶ About a third of all retail purchases are now made through the use of credit cards and bank customers had access to 7240 Automated Teller Machines (ATMs).

Personal finance commitments

Secured housing finance commitments to individuals

During 1995–96 there were housing finance commitments on 451 520 dwellings to the value of $43 679m. In addition there were loans of $3509m for alterations and additions to dwellings.

Purchase of motor cars and station wagons

During 1995–96 there were 129 715 commitments under fixed loan agreements for the purchase of new cars and station wagons, totalling $2505m, and 489 333 commitments for loans on used cars and station wagons, totalling $5558m.

Private donations

In the 12 months to August 1997, 76.4% of women and 67.5% of men made donations to support various community organisations. 30.2% of all persons did not make any donations.

Bankruptcies

Number of bankruptcies

During 1995–96 there were 17 362 bankruptcies, 4773 being business related (27.5%) and 12 589 non–business related. The rate of insolvency has risen sharply: there were 2947 business and 5546 non–business related bankruptcies in 1989–90.

Causes of bankruptcies

The principal cause for business related bankruptcies in 1995–96 was economic conditions, at 26.4%, compared with 25.1% in 1994–95. The second main cause was lack of business ability, 16.6% in 1995–6 compared with 9.1% the previous year. The major cause of non–business related bankruptcies were (a) absence of health insurance or extensive ill-health, (b) adverse litigation and (c) domestic discord.

AN OVERVIEW

In 1994–95 there were 922 800 businesses in Australia, of which 887 300 were small businesses.

- Manufacturing was responsible for 14.6% of GDP, the retail trade for 10.7% and property and business services 8.1%.
- Service industries were 63.8% of all businesses.

PRIMARY INDUSTRIES

Agricultural industries – overall statistics

The level of production and the value of the industry are subject to climatic conditions, overseas demand and the prices of agricultural exports. Despite drought conditions affecting grain production, 1994–95 saw a further recovery from the low point of 1991–92. Wool prices showed an improvement in 1994–95 with significant falls after the end of the year. Milk production and prices remained at 1993–94 levels. Cattle meat for slaughter continued a downward movement.

- In 1996–97 the gross value of agricultural production was $25 680m and gross farm product was 3% of GDP. Rural exports, of $20 398m, were 29% of the total value of Australia's merchandise exports.
- The estimated turnover of the agricultural industry in 1994–95 was $23 516.3m.
- Farm businesses had an average turnover of $219 200 in 1994–95, up 8.7% on the previous year.
- In 1994–95 the total value contributed to the Australian economy by the agricultural industry was $9768.1m.
- The average farm-business asset value at the end of 1994–95 was $1.139m.
- At current prices, the gross farm product rose from $10 367m in 1991–92 to $11 958m in 1993–94.

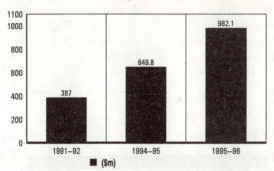

Industry Gross Product ($m): 1991–92: 387; 1994–95: 649.8; 1995–96: 982.1

▶ In 1994–95 the gross indebtedness of farm businesses was $18 267.7m, compared with $15 390.5m in 1992–93.

People in agricultural industries

A total of 421 900 people were employed in agricultural establishments in 1995–96.

▶ 230 100 were employers and self-employed, 165 000 were wage and salary earners and 26 800 were unpaid family helpers.

▶ 5.1% of Australia's labour force was employed in the agricultural sector.

Land use in the agricultural industry

The total area of Australian agricultural establishments in 1996 was 463.4 million ha compared with 463.3 million ha the previous year.

▶ Qld, with 148.1 million ha, had the greatest area of land being used for agricultural purposes.

▶ The sector with the greatest number of establishments was beef farming at 36 482 establishments; the second greatest was mixed grain–sheep/beef-cattle farming.

▶ 7266 beef-cattle establishments had an area of 1000 or more ha, of which 1110 had an area of 25 000 ha or more and 384 had an area of 200 000 ha or more.

Crops

In June 1789, 200 bushels of wheat, 35 bushels of barley and some oats, maize and flax were harvested at the government farm at Rose Hill (later Parramatta, NSW), the grain being stored as seed for the next season.

▶ The total area under cultivation for crops in 1995–96 was 17.03 million ha, down 5.61% on the 18.04 million ha of the previous year.

▶ All crops (excluding pastures and grasses) had a gross value of $10 490m in 1994–95.

In 1996–97, exports of major crops were worth $820m, a decline of 0.6% on the previous year.

Cereals for grain
Area of crop (in '000 hectares)

	1994	1995	1996
barley	3424	2479	3253
oats	947	897	1225
rice	129	119	140
wheat	8383	7891	9719

Wheat

▶ In 1996 WA had the greatest area under wheat, at 4.05 million ha; NSW had 2.48 million ha.

▶ WA produced 7.12 million t of wheat, NSW 4.66 million t and SA 2.88 million t.

▶ In 1995–96, 17.196 million t of wheat was produced in Australia, with a gross value of $4402m.

Rice

A bumper rice harvest was predicted for 1996–97 of 1.46 million t (paddy), an increase of 54% from 1995–96.

Legumes for grain

Legumes for grain (chickpeas, field peas, legumes) were grown on 1.37 million ha in 1996.

Other grains

In 1995–96, 687 000 ha were planted with grain sorghum, producing 1.27 million t, and 50 000 ha were planted with maize, producing 242 000 t.

▶ It is estimated that in 1997–98 Australian plantings of canola will be boosted by 51% to 565 000 ha and that production will rise to 822 000 t.

▶ Farmers have indicated that they intended to plant 8.79 million ha with wheat in 1996 and actually planted 9.74 million ha. They intended to plant 11.12 million ha in 1997.

Oilseeds
Area of crop (in '000 hectares)

	1994–95	1995–96	1996–97
canola	356.25	376.6	421.3
cottonseed	263.9	557.1	641.0
linseed	8.2	13.6	7.8
peanuts	14.2	22.7	25.1
safflower	30.3	40.1	36.0
soybeans	18.1	24.0	39.3
sunflower	136.1	82.8	136.9

Orchard fruit
Total number of trees (in '000s)

	1994	1995	1996
oranges	6597	6297	6583
lemons and limes	367	383	400
mandarins	601	729	889
apples	5033	5101	5230
pears (incl. nashi)	1797	1766	1703
apricots	646	642	629
nectarines	561	660	629
plums and prunes	863	907	912

Citrus

In 1994–95 the total citrus production was 612 kt compared with 567 kt in 1990–91, of which 245 kt was destined for fresh sales and 108 kt for export. In 1993–94, 443 kt were processed.

▶ In 1995–96, 12.4 ML of orange juice was exported, the domestic supply was 78 ML and 164.2 ML were imported. Imports have risen as a proportion of availability from 7.1% in 1988–89 to 67.8% in 1996–96.

Viticulture

The area of vines at harvest in 1995–96 was 82 600 ha, compared with 60 100 ha in 1990–91.

▶ 219 kt of red grapes, 328 kt of white grapes and 432 kt of multipurpose grapes were harvested.

▶ A total of 1212.4 kt by fresh weight of grapes were produced: 870.8 kt for winemaking and 471.7 kt for drying and table use.

▶ In 1997–98 the harvest was a record 954 000 t, an increase of 150 000 t over 1996–97. 1997–98 total intake of premium wine grapes was 646 000 t, compared with 500 000 t the previous year.

▶ There was a vineyard planting program of 25 500 ha in 1992–96.

▶ In 1997–98 the premium red grape harvest increased to 299 000 t, with premium red planting outpacing premium white.

▶ On the domestic market in 1995–96, 245.86 ML of table wine and 229.86 ML of sparkling wine were sold, as were 27 ML of sherry, port and other fortified wines and 1 ML of vermouth and other wines.

▶ 20.2 ML of wine were imported in 1995–96, compared with 9 ML in 1990–91.

▶ 129.81 ML of wine, worth $469.4m, were exported in 1995–96, compared with 57.04 ML, worth $175.7m, in 1990–91. The major destinations for wine exports in 1994–95 were the UK

Recipients of Australian wine, 12 months to April 1998

	volume in millions of litres (ML)	change %
United Kingdom	82.40	9.5
United States	31.33	48.9
New Zealand	21.62	41.0
Canada	7.56	16.7
Ireland	4.99	18.0
Japan	4.65	86.2
Germany	3.49	27.1
Norway	2.70	10.4
Netherlands	2.66	27.0
Switzerland	2.56	55.5
France	1.49	202.0

(52.48 ML), the USA (13.26 ML), New Zealand (14.46 ML), Sweden (8.08 ML) and Canada (5.35 ML). In 1997–98 the volume and value of wines approved for export exceeded all previous records, with an increase of 20.3% to a total of 185.24 ML.

Tropical fruit

Tropical fruit, total area cultivated (ha)

	1994	1995	1996
bananas	8756	8281	8835
pawpaws	399	320	319
pineapples	3668	3209	3077

▶ 218 700 t of bananas, 4894 t of pawpaws and 134 362 t of pineapples were produced in 1996.

Other fruit

In 1996, 391 t of raspberries and 10 957 t of strawberries were produced.

Vegetables for human consumption

A total area of 119 300 ha was given over in 1995–96 to the cultivation of vegetables for human consumption, the greatest area being that for potatoes at 37 600 ha, from which 1.22 million t were harvested.

Cotton

Cotton was grown on 245 000 ha in 1994–95 and from the seed cotton when ginned 474 000 t of cotton seed and 335 t of lint were produced. The yield was 3.2 t of seed cotton per ha compared with 2.7 t in the preceding year.

Sugar

Qld has about 95% of Australia's sugar production, with some 75% of the crop being harvested north of the Tropic of Capricorn. The remainder of sugar production principally comes from northern NSW. In 1996–97 an Australian total of 401 000 ha of sugar cane was harvested, producing 38.89 Mt of raw sugar cane for crushing. In NSW the yield of sugar cane for crushing in 1996–97 was 123 400 t per hectare and in Qld the yield was 95 900 t per hectare.

Livestock

The arrival of the First Fleet was accompanied by a small herd of cattle, all of which was soon lost, sheep which either strayed or died, and horses, only two of which survived for more than two years.

Cattle

In 1997 Australia's cattle herd numbered 26 354 000 head.

◗ 38.8% of all cattle were in Qld, 24.66% in NSW and 16.95% in Vic.

◗ In 1995–96 the total whole-milk intake by factories was 8716 ML, with a gross value of $2965.8m, compared with 6731 ML with a gross value of $1960m in 1991–92.

◗ 6.8 million head of cattle and 1 million head of calves were slaughtered for human consumption in 1995–96, producing 1.67 million t of beef and veal, with a gross value of $3474.3m.

◗ 738 kt of beef and veal were exported in 1995–96, with a value of $2385m.

Domesticated buffalo

There were estimated to be 10 900 domesticated buffalo in the NT in 1996.

Sheep

At 31 March 1996 the sheep and lamb flock was 126.32 million, an increase of 2.5% on the previous year. In 1989–90 Australian sheep numbers reached an all-time peak of 176.7 million, falling to 163.2 million in 1990–91.

◗ 34.68% of all sheep in 1996 were in NSW, 24.55% in WA and 17.89% in Vic.

◗ 1995 mating intentions at the beginning of the season were 51.9 million, there were 53.2 million actual matings and 59.6% of ewes

Cattle numbers (in '000s)

	1994	1995	1996	1997
milk cattle	2678	2740	2808	3067
beef cattle	23 080	22 991	23 569	23 297

Sheep numbers (in '000s)

	1994	1995	1996
sheep 1 year and over	102 831	95 926	95 315
lambs & hoggets under 1 year	29 739	27 284	31 000

were mated to merino rams.

▶ 13.9 million head of sheep and 14 million head of lambs were slaughtered for human consumption in 1995–96, producing 295 000 t of mutton and 260 000 t of lamb, with a gross value of $1005.5m.

▶ 141 kt of mutton and 52 kt of lamb were exported in 1995–96, valued at $496m.

In 1995–96 the total production of all red meats was 2.586 million t.

Wool production

In 1995–96, 143.2 million sheep were shorn, with an average fleece weight of 4.8 kg. Shorn wool weighed a total 641.4 t, with a total wool gross value of $4686.8m. The effect of decreased sheep numbers and a decline in the wool price is illustrated by the comparison with the 1990–91 figures, of 212.9 million sheep and lambs shorn with a total wool weight of 1 066 100 t and a gross value of $4181m.

▶ In 1996 there were 1.7 million bales in Wool International's closing stocks compared with 3.1 million bales in 1994.

▶ The average auction price per kg of wool in 1997 was 397 cents per kg compared with 370 cents per kg in 1996 and 503 cents per kg in 1994.

Live sheep and cattle exports

During 1995–96 live cattle exports reached 616 800 head, with a gross value of $344.03m, compared with the 1990–91 figure of 94 900 head and a gross value of $50.41m. Live sheep exports in 1995–96 were 5.41 million head with a gross value of $189m, compared with 3.19 million head and a gross value of $46m in 1990–91.

Pigs

Pig numbers (in '000s)

1994	1995	1996
2775	2653	2663

▶ In 1996, 26.92% of pigs were in NSW, 25.15% in Qld and 17.39% in Vic.

▶ 4.8 million pigs were slaughtered for human consumption in 1995–96, producing 329 000 t of pig meat, with a gross value of $589.2m.

Poultry

In 1996 there were 65.59 million chickens in Australia, 17% were hens and pullets for egg production and 83% were meat strain (broiler chickens). There were about 2.09 million other poultry, of which about 22.11% were ducks and 59.82% were turkeys.

▶ During 1995–96, 329.3 million chickens, 9.5 million other fowls and turkeys and 2.6 million ducks and drakes were slaughtered for human consumption. The total dressed weight of all chickens was 468 000 t and of all other poultry 503 t. The gross value of all poultry slaughtered was $964.6m.

Beekeeping

In 1996 there were 1659 beekeepers with 534 000 beehives, 381 000 of the hives being productive. They produced 25 990 t of honey with an average production per hive of 683 g; 620 t of beeswax was also collected.

Timber industry

Employment in forest product industries

In 1993–94, 44 000 persons were employed in the wood and wood products industry, a marked decline from the 50 500 employees of 1987–88. The paper and paper products industry employed 61 300 persons in 1993–94, compared with 73 000 in 1987–88.

Production, trade and consumption of sawnwood

In 1995–96 there was a total production of 3 433 000 m^3 of sawnwood, comprising 1 456 000 m³ of broadleaf (hardwood) and 2 655 000 m³ of coniferous (softwood).

▶ Total consumption of sawnwood was 4 121 000 m³ compared with 4 698 000 m³ the previous year.

Exports of sawnwood

A total of 53 800 m³ of sawnwood timber was exported in 1995–96 to a value of $39.9m.

▶ 32 258 m³ went to Asian countries, 12 711 m³ to Europe, 3773 m³ to New Zealand and 3430 m³ to the USA.

Imports of sawnwood

In the year 1996–97 there were imports of 742 000 m³, worth $373.8m; the corresponding figures for 1989–90 were 1 407 000 m³ and $463.5m.

▶ 332 000 m³ were imported from New Zealand in 1996–97, and 142 000 m³ from the USA.

Production and trade in railway sleepers

There has been a marked decline in the use of timber for railway sleepers, due to a large extent to a dwindling timber resource and the increased use of concrete sleepers. In 1995–96, 85 000 m³ of timber sleepers were produced compared with 132 000 m³ in 1988–89. In 1992–93, 8000 m³ of sleepers were exported, but in 1995–96 exports were zero.

Fisheries

The area of the Australian fishing zone, including the offshore territories of Cocos (Keeling), Christmas, Norfolk, Macquarie, Heard and McDonald islands, is 8.94 million km². More than 3000 species of marine and freshwater fish are present in Australian waters, as are an equal number of molluscs and crustacea. Less than 100 of these species are exploited commercially. In 1993 the total world catch from zones adjacent to Australia was 12 598 kt. The fishing industry is one of Australia's most important rural activities. In 1976–77 the gross value of fisheries production was $206m; by 1994–95 it had risen to $1745m.

Destination and value of exports of fishery products

1994–95 exports of fishery products were worth $1358m compared with $1085m in 1992–93. Japan was the biggest customer, at 40.9%, followed by Hong Kong at 19.8% and Taiwan at 14.9%.

◗ Exports of rock lobster (crayfish) were valued at $416.5m in 1995–96, prawns at $223m and abalone at $147.5m. Tuna to the value of $55.4m was exported, mainly for the Japanese sashimi market.

Source and value of imports of fishery products

1994–95 imports of marine products were valued at $666m compared with $529m in 1992–93. Thailand provided 24.9% of the imports, followed by New Zealand with 17.6% and the USA 7.2%.

Imports of seafood totalled 68 923 t in 1996–97, comprising 47 879 t of fresh, chilled or frozen fish, 3010 t of smoked, dried or salted fish, 26 976 t of canned fish and 5258 t of other fish preparations, and 1563 t of canned crustaceans and molluscs. Canned tuna was 11 140 t and canned salmon 8718 t.

◗ Canned fish imports were worth $116.59m in 1996–97, and canned crustacea and molluscs $13.58m.

◗ Imports of canned tuna were valued at $41.45m and imports of canned prawns were valued at $1.76m.

Aquaculture

Aquaculture makes a major contribution to Australia's fisheries production, both from farmed fish and the production of a variety of shellfish. The value of aquaculture production has increased from $255.5m in 1992–93 to $388.1m in 1995–96.

◗ Farmed fish, including salmon, tuna and trout, brought in $115.9m.

◗ Crustaceans, mainly prawns, were worth $36.1m.

- Molluscs contributed $186.2m, pearl oysters' share was $131.3m and edible oysters' share $52m.

Manufacturing

As at June 1996 manufacturing establishments in Australia employed 923 100 persons, paid $29 902m in wages for the year ended June 1996 and had a turnover of $197 963m.

- Employment in manufacturing fell by 0.1% in 1995–96, with the greatest decrease being 7% in the ACT.
- There were significant increases in employment in the NT (+12%), Tas. (+2%) and Vic. (+1%).
- NSW had the highest number of persons employed in manufacturing in June 1996, at 303 500, then came Vic. with 294 500 and Qld with 137 300.
- The industry subdivisions with the largest percentage decrease in employment for the year were wood and paper product manufacturing (–4%) and non-metallic mineral product manufacturing (–3%).
- Employment in metal product manufacturing and machinery and equipment manufacturing was up 1% in both cases.
- In NSW machinery and equipment manufacturing, with 62 700, had the greatest number of employees, followed by metal product manufacturing with 52 400. In Vic. the machinery and equipment industry subdivision with 73 200 had the greatest group of employees nationwide. The textile, clothing, footwear and leather manufacturing and the metal product manufacturing subdivisions each employed 36 700 persons. Turnover in Australian manufacturing establishments in current prices increased by $6273m (3%) in 1995–96.
- Prices for manufactured goods grew by 2.4% over the year implying a real turnover growth of about 1% compared to 1994–95.

Sales and trading profits

In 1995–96 manufacturing industries in Australia had total sales of goods and services of $204 191m; the cost of sales was $141 701m, giving a profit of $62 490m.

Employment

In 1995–96 23.8% of workers in the manufacturing industry were employed in businesses employing less than 20 people, 26.2% were employed in businesses employing 20–99 people, and 50% were employed in businesses employing 100 or more people.

In August 1997, 65.4% of male workers in manufacturing had been born in Australia compared with a proportion of the total male civilian population of 75.4%.

State and territory employment in manufacturing

As at 30 June 1996, 298 000 people were employed in manufacturing activities in NSW, 292 000 in Vic., 134 000 in Qld, 86 000 in SA and 69 000 in WA. 30 000 were employed in Tas., the NT and the ACT.

Proportion of employment by manufacturing industries, 1997

	%
machinery and equipment	22.7
food, beverage and tobacco	16.1
metal products	15.3
printing, publishing and recorded media	11.3
textile, clothing and footwear	9.0
petroleum, coal, chemical and associated products	8.8
other	16.8

Manufacturing industry gross product, 1995–96

	$bn
NSW	21.0
Vic.	19.7
Qld	8.5
SA	5.9
WA	4.2
Tas.	1.8
NT	0.3
ACT	0.2

Manufacturing value added, as % of GDP, in 1993

	%
Australia	**14.4**
France	19.5
Germany	26.2
Italy	20.2
Japan	26.8
Netherlands	17.6
Sweden	18.0
United Kingdom	18.1
United States	18.0

Manufacturing employment, as % of total civilian population

	%
Australia	**13.2**
Canada	14.4
France	19.0
Germany	25.6
Japan	23.2
New Zealand	15.8
Sweden	17.3
United Kingdom	18.0
United States	16.0

Textiles, clothing and footwear (TCF) industries

TCF manufacturing is broad and diverse, covering wool scouring and top making (tops are continuous strands of untwisted fibres from which shorter fibres are removed by combing), leather tanning, spinning, weaving, knitting, design and fabrication of clothing, leather and shoes, plus textiles such as towels, blankets, sheets and curtains. The industry also has inputs into other industries, such as furniture, motor vehicles, hospitality and health services.

- Employment in TCF manufacturing industries has declined. There are about 100 000 recorded TCF manufacturing jobs. This is about 1% of total employment and 9% of manufacturing employment.
- Between May 1985 and May 1997 16 000 formal jobs were lost in metropolitan areas and 25 000 additional jobs were created in regional areas.
- The TCF sector is characterised by having an ageing workforce with a

significant non–English speaking background.

▶ It has been estimated that homeworking in the clothing industry in 1997 was the equivalent of about 23 000 full-time jobs. Although homeworking provides a more flexible labour force concerns have been expressed about working conditions.

SCIENCE AND TECHNOLOGY

From May to August in 1770, Joseph Banks and Carl Solander, members of James Cook's expedition, were the first Europeans to begin the identification and study of Australian flora and fauna. In 1788 George Caley began systematically collecting plants for Joseph Banks, and was one of the first Europeans to study the reproduction of marsupials. In 1801 a French scientific expedition led by Nicolas Baudin began a three-year hydrographic survey of the coastline.

The Philosophical Society of Australasia, founded on 27 June 1821, was the colony's first scientific organisation. The Commonwealth Scientific and Industrial Research Organisation (CSIRO) was established as an independent statutory authority in 1949. CSIRO carries out scientific research for the benefit of the community, industry and for national objectives, and it encourages or facilitates the application or utilisation of the results of its research.

Research and development (R&D)

Human resources devoted to R&D in 1995–96 was estimated to be 26 570 person years, up 3% on 1994–95.

Business expenditure on R&D (BERD)

Australian BERD is relatively low by

international standards, being 0.74% of GDP in 1994–95, compared with Sweden (2.32%) or Japan (1.94%). 1995–96 expenditure on BERD was estimated to be $4243m, up 22% on 1994–95. BERD as a percentage of GDP was 0.87% compared with 0.76% the previous year, with expenditure up 74% in the mining sector and 26% in manufacturing.

❱ The business sector provided 92% of the 1995–96 funding, overseas funding provided 3% and the Commonwealth government 2%.

Higher education expenditure on R&D (HERD)

Expenditure on HERD was estimated to be $2039m in 1995, with HERD as a percentage of GDP being 0.42% compared with 0.4% in 1994.

❱ 48% of principal HERD expenditure was directed toward the advancement of knowledge, 25% to the study of society, and 22% to medicine and health science.

Computers

As at June 1994, 49.5% of Australia's non-agricultural employing businesses had computers. These businesses accounted for 83% of total employment. Among the industry sectors, electricity, gas and water supply had an 86% computer usage, for the property and business sector 73%, finance 71%. The usage for the retail trade industry was 27%.

❱ Businesses with computers employed 4.3 million people, with 1.6 million being regular users.

❱ Almost all businesses employing more than 100 employees had computers. 46% of businesses employing 1–19 persons had computers.

❱ In June 1994 among businesses there were 1 524 000 work stations, including 1.05 million personal computers.

Computers in Australian homes

A February 1994 survey found that about 23% of all Australian households were using a computer. Married couples with dependent families had the highest usage at 38.1%. 742 000 households with a home-based business had a computer.

▶ 80 000 home-based businesses had a modem allowing access to computers and facilities at a distance from the home.

▶ For all homes with a computer use given was educational purposes (24.9%) followed by entertainment (22.5%).

Computer services industry

At 30 June 1993 there were 4894 computer services businesses, employing 30 062 persons and earning a gross income of $2763.8m. The largest sector of the industry was computer consultancy services, which had 4323 businesses and 22 509 employees.

ENERGY

Energy consumption in Australia has increased about 2% per annum for the last 20 years. The energy sector contributes about 5% to GDP, 16% to total export income and more than 2% to employment.

Household expenditure on fuel and power

In 1993–94 the average household spent $15.92 per week on fuel and power.

Household energy sources by consumption in Australia

	%	
	1974–75	1995–96
electricity	32.3	42.5
natural gas	11.4	29.1
wood	29.0	22.8
heating oil	13.2	1.0
solar energy	0.1	0.9
other*	13.9	3.7

* mainly coal and petroleum products

Coal gas

The Australian Gas Light Company

held its first meeting in Sydney in 1836. On 24 May 1841 the first street gas lamps were in use in Sydney utilising the company's reticulated supply. By 1918–19 there were 135 gas and coke works throughout Australia with 5495 employees. The use of coal gas has now been replaced by natural gas.

Natural gas

There were 76 352 km of pipes in the natural gas reticulation and transmission system in 1994–95, an increase of 2.2% over 1993–94. There were 2.8 million customers and sales yielded $2350m.

Electricity

Mainland Australia does not have many rivers suitable for hydro-electricity generation other than the Snowy Mountains Hydro-Electric Scheme in NSW. Most of the electricity generated in the eastern states is produced by coal-burning power stations situated near major coalfields, e.g. the Hunter Valley (NSW) and the Latrobe Valley (Vic.).

◗ Hydro-electricity is the main source of electricity in Tas. An even distribution of rainfall throughout the year and many dams in the central highlands provide the water storage capacity allowing the state to produce Australia's cheapest electricity.

◗ Since the beginning of the 1990s the national electricity generation capacity has increased by almost 5000 MW.

◗ In the same period the number of customers served by electricity businesses has increased from 7.27 million to 7.92 million. 960 000 are commercial and industrial customers.

◗ Power consumption rose from 126 155 million kW hours in 1991 to 140 272 million kW hours in 1995.

◗ In the year ended 30 June 1994 the principal fuels consumed in power stations were 44.90 million t of brown coal, 39.03 million t of black coal and 151 440t of oil.

▶ Electricity was passing along 754 529 km of overhead lines and 57 512 km of underground cable at 30 June 1996.

▶ Income from the sales of electricity totalled $12 343.28m in the year ended 30 June 1995.

▶ As at 30 June 1995 there were 42 151 personnel employed in the electricity industry compared with 61 941 in 1991.

Energy exports

For the year 1994–95 energy products were worth 16% of Australia's exports. About 70% of all energy products are exported, with coal the leading product with 10% of total exports.

Renewable sources of energy

In Australia the use of renewable energy for the short and medium future offers remote areas one of the best prospects for power supply. More than 300 communities and 10 000 households generate their own electricity, using renewable energy technologies.

Solar energy

The use of solar energy to generate power is by photovoltaics or solar thermal technologies. Telstra uses photovoltaic cells to provide the power supply in rural and remote areas. Solar thermal technologies are employed in the production of electricity, for space heating and water heating. At 30 June 1994, 300 000 (5%) of Australian homes had solar water heaters, with the NT having 58% of these.

Wind

The coastal regions of southern Australia are the best areas for the location of wind farms, a promising and low-cost alternative for electricity generation which could provide 10% or more of the nation's needs. As at 30 June 1995, 6539 kW were generated by wind power, principally in Vic.and WA.

Wood
Each year Australia uses about 6 million t of wood for industrial boilers and dryers, metallurgical processes, cooking and home heating. The main sources are forestry residues, sawlogs, pulplogs and at times forest logging.

Bagasse
Bagasse, the fibrous residue left from the production of sugar, is used as fuel in the sugar mills of NSW and Qld. After wood it is the second largest renewable energy source in Australia.

Ethanol
Ethanol traditionally is produced from expensive feedstocks, e.g. grains and sugars. Research is being conducted into the use of low-cost feedstocks, e.g. forestry waste, sawdust, cereal straws, cotton trash and tree trimmings for ethanol production. Ethanol is a useful partial alternative for lead in petrol and has the potential to reduce lead in the atmosphere and greenhouse emissions. Throughout NSW and Vic. there are more than 90 service stations selling a petrol–ethanol blend.

TRANSPORT

Shipping
Any Australian vessel over 24 m in length must be registered. As at 30 June 1996 there were 4720 recreational vessels, 2130 fishing vessels, 32 government vessels, 17 foreign-owned vessels chartered to an Australian operator and 944 vessels used for commercial purposes. The number of Australian-registered trading vessels has declined sharply in recent years. In December 1971 there were 133 vessels of 200 gross t or more on the Australian register, but at 30 June 1995 there were only 85 vessels of 150 gross t or more. However, the total gross tonnage of Australian-registered vessels has

increased from 1 004 832 gross t in 1971 to 2 298 894 gross t in 1995.

▶ Australia's coastal fleet numbered 43 vessels of a total 822 416 gross tonnage. Three vessels were overseas-owned but Australian-registered and three vessels were overseas-owned and overseas-registered.

Coastal cargo

During 1994–95, 49.19 million t of cargo were loaded and 50.46 million t were discharged at Australian ports as part of the coastal trade. In 1995–96, 41 ports were visited by coastal shipping.

Maritime safety

During 1995–95, 1108 persons were rescued in incidents, with the rescue operations coordinated by the Maritime Research Coordination Committee.

Road transport
The road system

At 30 June 1996 there were 306 187 km of bitumen or concrete roads and 263 813 km of gravel, crushed stone or other improved surface roads in Australia.

▶ There had been an increase of 5.71% in the length of bitumen or concrete roads since 30 June 1990.

Vehicle registrations

At 31 May 1995 there were 10 650 902 motor vehicles (excluding motor cycles, plant and equipment, caravans and trailers) on register in Australia. Between 30 June 1993 and 30 June 1995 there had been 1 153 358 new registrations.

▶ There were 296 628 motor cycles registered in 1995 compared with 366 878 in 1982.

▶ 1.53 million light commercial vehicles, 337 421 rigid trucks, 58 322 articulated trucks, 46 971 non–freight carrying trucks, 52 170 buses, 101 195 plant and equipment, 265 374 caravans and 1.74 million trailers were also registered.

▶ In 1990–91, 542 454 new motor vehicles (excluding motor cycles)

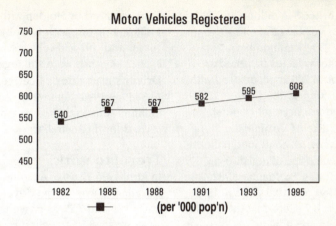

Motor Vehicles Registered (per '000 pop'n)

1982: 540
1985: 567
1988: 567
1991: 582
1993: 595
1995: 606

were registered; for 1995–96 the figure was 636 529, an increase of 14.7%. New passenger vehicle registrations in the same period rose by 18.97% and registrations of new motor cycles by 8.22%.

Vehicles and population

There were 567 vehicles per 1000 of population in 1988 and 606 in 1995, a rise of 6.43%.

▶ The highest rate of vehicle ownership was WA at 679 per 1000 of population and the lowest the NT at 520 per 1000 of population.

Type of fuel

Vehicles using leaded petrol outnumbered those using unleaded petrol by 5.97 million to 3.63 million at 30 June 1993 and 5.31 million to 4.61 million at 30 June 1995.

Distance travelled

For the year ended 30 September 1995 it was estimated that Australian motor vehicles travelled a total distance of 166 514 million km, with passenger vehicles travelling the most, at 123 691 million km.

▶ Passenger vehicles travelled an average of 14 700 km compared with the 89 900 km travelled by articulated trucks (semi-trailers).

Average age of vehicles

There has been a continued increase in the average age of registered vehicles. It was 7.6 years in 1982, 9.8 years in 1991 and 10.6 years in 1995.

▶ Buses, at 8.9 years, had the lowest average age and non–freight carrying trucks the highest at 13.7 years. Passenger vehicles had an average age of 10.4 years.

Predominant colours of motor vehicles

At 30 June 1993, 31.8% of Australian passenger vehicles were white, 14.3% were blue, 13.3% were red and 7% were green.

Make of vehicle

In 1995, of passenger vehicles registered, 1 946 343 were made by Ford, followed by Holden with 1 826 559, Toyota with 1 407 215 and Nissan with 791 538 vehicles.

▶ 6622 Leylands were still registered.

Driver's and rider's licences

At 30 June 1996 there were 12.121 million licensed drivers and motor cycle riders in Australia.

Travel to work

In April 1996 77.6% of Australians travelled to work as the driver of a car or van and 7.2% as passengers in a car or van. 8.5% travelled by train, 7.1% by bus and 1.3% by motor cycle. 2.8% used a bicycle and 6.3% walked. Some used a combination of modes of transport.

Household expenditure on transport

In 1993–94 the average household spent $83.88 a week on transport.

Road safety

In 1972 on Australian roads there were 26.59 fatalities per 100 000 of population, a rate which had fallen to 11.17 in 1995. For April 1997 the national road toll was 129 compared with 168 in April 1996. The number of people killed on roads rose steadily from 2598 in 1963 until it peaked at 3705 in 1978. Factors such as better roads, vehicle safety design features, the compulsory wearing of seat belts, the fitting of airbags, random breath testing and the police use of red-light cameras and speed cameras have contributed to a marked decline in fatalities.

- There were 1411 male and 562 female deaths.
- Of those killed, 871 were drivers, 501 passengers, 349 pedestrians, 193 motor cyclists, and 58 bicyclists.

Factors affecting road fatalities

Age plays a significant role in road fatalities. Of all those persons killed on the roads in 1996, 1002 (50.8%) were aged 17–39 years. There were 140 fatal crashes involving articulated trucks in 1996, a decline of 13.6% on the previous year. Buses were involved in 31 fatal crashes in 1996, a rise of 40.9% on the previous year. In 1981 44% of driver and rider fatalities had prohibited blood alcohol levels. By 1990 the figure had fallen to 34%. In 1994 it had fallen further to 28% but rose again to 30% in 1995.

Fatality rates by state and territories

The fatality rates vary between the states and territories. In 1997–98 the NT had the highest rate of road fatalities per 100 000 population, at 32.06, compared with the ACT at 5.49. The overall rate for Australia was 9.5.

Characteristics of fatal crashes

Of those killed on the roads in 1996–97, 871 were drivers, 501 passengers, 349 pedestrians, 193 motor cyclists and 58 bicyclists. In 1997–98, 35.5% of fatalities occurred with vehicles travelling at up to 60 km/h, 17.2% of vehicles were travelling at 65–95 km/h and the remainder at higher speeds.

- 57.5% of fatalities happened during the daytime and 42.5% at night. 59.6% occurred on a weekday and 40.4% at the weekend.
- Between July 97–June 98 there were 1873 road fatalities, compared with 1765 the previous year, an increase of 6.1%, when there had been 1228 male and 537 female deaths.
- In 1996 there were 1973 road fatalities, compared with 2017 the previous year, a decline of 2.2%. Of the 1996 deaths, 1411 were male and 562 female.

Alcohol and road crashes

If a blood alcohol content of 0.05 g of alcohol per 100 ml blood or more is taken as a measure of intoxication, a minimum of 500 fatalities are caused by drunk driving each year.

Hospitalisation

During 1994, 22 154 people were hospitalised as a result of road crashes. Between 1992 and 1994 there was an increase of 3% in those hospitalised.

- 13% of those in fatal accidents had been intoxicated, compared with 7% of serious injury cases.
- 25% of fatal crashes were at intersections, contrasted with 40% of hospitalisation crashes.
- Persons hospitalised as a result of road accidents fell by 22% during 1989–94, with the most marked decreases being bicyclists (down 31%) and passengers (down 27%).

Cost of road crashes

It was estimated that in 1993 road crashes cost Australia $6.1bn, the average fatality costing $752 400.

Railways

On 26 September 1855 Australia's first steam railway was opened, covering the 14 miles between Sydney and Parramatta (NSW). Today there are state government systems in NSW, Vic., Qld and WA, plus the National Rail Corporation and the Australian National Railways Commission.

▶ In 1995 government railways operated over 36 026 route-km.

▶ Government railways provided about 425 million suburban passenger journeys and 9.9 million country passenger journeys in 1994–95.

▶ During 1994–95, 214.99 million t of freight were carried on government railways compared with 185.53 million t in 1989–90, freight earnings being $2880.36m in 1994–95 compared with $2421.21m in 1989–90.

Non-government railways

Non-government railways exceeding 2 km carried 146 million t in 1994–95, including 97.3 million t of iron ore, 34.4 million t of sugar and 5.7 million t of coal.

Major railway disasters

▶ On 20 April 1908 a collision with a stationary train caused 44 deaths at Sunshine, Melbourne.

▶ Track faults caused the derailment of a commuter train at Granville, Sydney, on 18 January 1977. The overhead road bridge was brought down on the train; 83 people were killed and 80 injured.

Level-crossing accidents

Level-crossing accidents are frequent occurrences, being principally due to the vehicle driver's negligence. The most serious level-crossing accidents have involved buses.

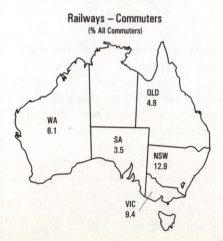

Railways – Commuters (% All Commuters)

QLD 4.8
WA 6.1
SA 3.5
NSW 12.9
VIC 9.4

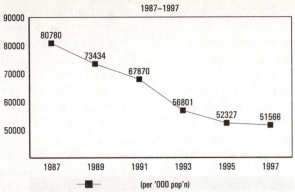

Railway Employed Persons
1987–1997

- 1987: 80780
- 1989: 73434
- 1991: 67870
- 1993: 56801
- 1995: 52327
- 1997: 51566

(per '000 pop'n)

▶ On 8 May 1943 near Wodonga (Vic.) 25 people were killed when a train struck a bus carrying service personnel.

▶ The negligence of the bus driver on 24 February 1951 caused the level-crossing collision with a train at Horsham (Vic.), killing 11 people.

Tramways

In October 1862 a horse tramway 2.4 km long was opened for traffic in Sydney, and on 15 September 1879 a steam tramway commenced operations in the same city. On 25 February 1961 the tramway system was closed down in Sydney when the last tram ran from La Perouse to the Randwick workshops. At present trams run regular services in Melbourne and Adelaide. Melbourne has a comprehensive tramway network extending over 332 km. The Glenelg line in Adelaide runs for a distance of 18 km. In 1997 Sydney reintroduced a privately owned light rail system in the inner city.

Monorail services

A privately owned monorail system links Sydney's central business district with the Darling Harbour complex. Units travel on a continuous elevated 3.6 km track at a normal top speed of 33 km/h. With nine units on the track the system has a capacity to move 7000 people per hour.

Air transport

The American magician Harry Houdini (Ehrich Weiss) made the first heavier-than-air flight in Australia at Diggers' Rest, Vic., on 18 March 1910, in a Voisin machine. Australia's first airmail delivery, of 1785 letters, was carried between Melbourne and Sydney by Maurice Gillaux in a Bleriot monoplane between 16 and 18 June 1914, taking 2½ days.

Licensed aerodromes

In 1995–96 there were 260 aerodromes licensed in Australia. Until 1997 the Federal Airports Commission (FAC) controlled 19 airports, of which seven handled international as well as domestic passengers. In 1995 these airports ranged from Mt Isa (Qld), with a staff of two, handling 73 000 passengers a year, to Kingsford Smith Airport, Sydney, with 345 employees handling more than 17 million passengers a year.

During 1997 the Commonwealth government began the sale of the airports, with the exception of Kingsford Smith Airport, where among other matters the disputes over aircraft noise have to be resolved.

- In the year to 30 June 1996 the airports handled 12 717 998 international passengers and 45 951 080 domestic passengers.
- There were 792 730 regular

passenger transport aircraft movements and 2 369 670 total aircraft movements.

- Kingsford Smith (Sydney) Airport was the busiest in terms of passengers handled, with 6 352 518 international and 13 684 518 domestic passengers.
- Bankstown (NSW), a general aviation airport, was the busiest in terms of aircraft movements, at 376 427.
- 43 international airlines and 10 dedicated freight services used Australian airports in the year ended June 1996.

Licensed pilots and engineers

As at 30 June 1996 there were 31 825 pilots with current Australian pilot's licences and 5444 licensed aircraft maintenance engineers.

- 29 879 medical certificates were issued to pilots and air traffic staff.

Number of registered aircraft

In 1995–96 there were 9689 aircraft contained in the Register of Australian Aircraft, not including gliders or ultralight aircraft registered by the Australian Ultralight Federation. There were 708 helicopters and 252 hot-air balloons in the Register, and there were 1209 gliders and 2900 ultralight aircraft.

Air safety record

Australian aviation has a very high reputation for air safety, principally due to high maintenance standards, low traffic density and generally favourable weather.

- In 1995 there were 273 aircraft accidents, with 51 fatalities, compared with 344 accidents and 81 fatalities in 1990.
- The highest death toll was in the crash of a Fokker Friendship at Mackay (Qld) on 10 June 1960, with 29 fatalities.

Australia's major airlines
Qantas

Qantas Airways Ltd, founded in the Qld outback in 1920, is the world's second oldest airline and the oldest in the English-speaking world. Formerly wholly owned by the Commonwealth government, the company was floated on the Australian Stock Exchange on 22 June 1995. British Airways had previously purchased 25% of Qantas on 10 March 1993.

- It has a core fleet of 97 aircraft, mainly Boeing 737s, 747s and 767s, and its subsidiary regional airlines operate a mixed fleet of 52 aircraft.
- Australia's leading domestic airline, Qantas is the world's 11th largest airline in terms of Revenue Passenger Kilometres (RPKs). The airline operates an average of 565 flights a day to 55 Australian destinations. It also operates about 370 international flights each week from Australia, to 51 destinations in 29 countries.
- In 1997, 30 800 staff were employed across its network.
- In 1997 Qantas carried 6 698 000 passengers on international flights and 9 622 000 passengers on domestic flights.
- In 1995–96 revenue increased by 2.5% to $4bn and Qantas had a profit after tax of $151.4m.
- Qantas's catering subsidiary supplies about 20 million meals a year and employs 2600 staff in catering centres in Sydney, Melbourne, Brisbane, Perth and Adelaide.

Ansett Australia

Founded by Reginald Ansett, the airline's first commercial flight was from Melbourne to Hamilton (Vic.), on 23 December 1936. Now 50% owned by Air New Zealand and 50% by the media group News Ltd, Ansett Australia is Australia's second major airline.

- In 1996 Ansett had a fleet of 81 aircraft and carried 12.16 million passengers and 113 340 t of cargo. In its second year as an international carrier it carried over 400 000 international passengers.

- In October 1997 Ansett Australia serviced routes to 11 destinations in Asia and New Zealand.
- Ansett Australia and its subsidiaries fly to 90 airports in Australia utilising 69 aircraft.
- Ansett Australia had a profit after tax of $58.4m in 1995–96.

TOURISM AND THE HOSPITALITY INDUSTRY

Tourism is one of the world's largest activities. Directly and indirectly it accounted for one in nine jobs and $A4500bn in world output in 1995. In August 1996 it was estimated that up to 25% of Australians might travel overseas in the next six months, 80% purely on holiday. Up to 40% may travel domestically in the following three months, 63% of whom would be using commercial lodging.

International inbound tourism

In the 12 months to 30 September 1997 there were 3 980 900 visitors aged 15 years and over to Australia. Japanese were the largest group (761 500), then came New Zealanders (615 800), UK people (366 500) and other Europeans (319 500).

- 2 332 100 came to Australia on holiday, 722 500 to visit relatives or friends, 427 100 on business and 489 200 for other purposes, e.g. education.
- In 1995, 30.7% of the inbound visitors stayed for less than one week, 31.1% stayed for one–two weeks and 18.1% stayed for two weeks–one month.
- NSW was the most popular state or territory, with 37% of the inbound visitor nights.
- Kingsford Smith (Sydney) Airport received 33.5% of inbound overseas visitors in the December quarter of 1996, Tullamarine (Melbourne) 3.3%, Eagle Farm (Brisbane) 37.3%, Cairns (Qld) 21.7% and Perth 3.3%.

Tourist expenditure by overseas visitors

It was estimated that in 1993–94 foreign visitors spent $10 640m dollars in Australia.

◗ $3700m was spent on air fares, $2300m on accommodation (including meals), and $1710m on other goods and services.

◗ Overseas visitors coming to Australia on package tours paid $1.2bn to Australian inbound tour operators in 1994–95. In 1996–97 39% of visitors came on a fully inclusive, pre-paid package tour, spending an average of $3435 while they were in Australia, compared with the average expenditure of $3955 by independent visitors.

◗ In 1995 the average overseas visitor spent $1936 in Australia. Indonesian visitors were the highest spenders per head at $3409, of which $260 was spent on entertainment and gambling. Japanese were the lowest, at $1410 per head.

◗ Overseas business visitors spent an average of $2147, while those on holiday spent $1631.

Top 10 regions visited by overseas tourists

Sydney was the most popular region visited in 1994, with 60.4% of international visitors, then the Gold Coast (Qld) (27.2%), Melbourne (26%) and Cairns (Qld) (19.1%).

Koalas and tourism

A survey was carried out in 1995 to assess the contribution of koalas to the Australian tourism industry.

◗ Nature-based activities are a major attraction for foreign tourists. 22% nominated Australia's unique wildlife as a factor influencing their decision to visit.

◗ 72% nominated koalas as the animal they particularly wanted to see, along with kangaroos (66%).

◗ 70% of departing tourists said they had actually seen a koala.

◗ It was estimated that foreign

tourists spent an estimated $336m per annum viewing koalas and buying 'koalabilia'.

Australian outward-bound tourists

In 1995, 2 518 600 Australians travelled abroad compared with 2 169 900 in 1990, a rise of 13.84%.

▶ The number of inbound visitors has consistently outnumbered outgoing Australians throughout the 1990s. Tourism has therefore provided a net positive contribution to Australia's balance of payments.

▶ Australian tourists travel to many destinations, the most commonly visited being New Zealand (14.7%), USA (12.5%) and the United Kingdom (10.5%).

▶ 42.48% of Australians travelled overseas on holiday, 25.6% visited friends/relatives and 17.42% were on business.

▶ When they travelled abroad, 10.8% of Australians intended to stay away under one week, 24.4% for one–two weeks, 26.6% for two weeks–one month and 18.2% for one–two months.

Domestic tourism

In 1995 Australians spent 27.1 million visitor nights within Australia for business reasons, 103.7 million nights on holiday and 74 million nights visiting friends and relatives.

▶ In the December quarter of 1995 there were 16.3 million domestic trips undertaken by Australians; 4.1 million trips were interstate and 12.2 million were intrastate trips.

▶ Friends' or relatives house/flat was the most popular form of accommodation (43% of total visitor nights), followed by hotel/motel facilities (20%).

▶ The most popular mode of transport was the private vehicle (77%), then aircraft (12%) and bus/coach (5%).

Tourist expenditure by Australian residents

It was estimated that Australian residents spent $36 300m on tourism in 1993–94.

- $5600m was spent on fuel (self drive), $5300m on domestic air fares and $3350m on accommodation.
- In February 1997, 86 700 households intended to go on a holiday worth $500 or more within the next 12 months.

Australia's tourist accommodation

During the six months to 31 December 1996 tourist accommodation projects to a value of $343m had been completed, including 2480 hotel and motel rooms (1717 of five-star grading), 128 holiday flats, units and serviced apartments and 569 backpacker hostel bed spaces.
- As at 30 March 1996 there were 173 876 rooms available in hotels, motels and guest houses compared with 169 630 the previous year. The occupancy rate was 59.9%.
- There were 42 186 holiday flats, units and houses available for tourists with an occupancy rate of 54%.
- At the same time there were 30 208 sites and cabins available at caravan parks with an occupancy rate of 46.4%.
- The average takings per room/night occupied in hotels, motels and guest houses rose from $92 in March 1995 to $96 a year later.
- Overseas visitors accounted for 23% of the room/nights in hotels, motels and guest houses.
- There was a total of 35.26 million guest nights in 1994–95; 39.92% were intrastate guests, 37.19% were interstate visitors and 22.89% were overseas guests.
- 36.8 million room/nights were sold in hotels, motels and guest houses in 1996, an increase of 2.5% on 1995.
- Total domestic and international visitor nights are estimated to increase at an average annual rate of 3.15% to reach 452.2 million in 2005, with the total nights spent in hotels, motels and guest houses to grow at 3.6% per annum from 69.2 million to 98.7 million.

Backpackers

In the year ended 30 September 1997 there were 281 700 backpackers in Australia who had visited more than one state or territory: 81% visited NSW, 69% Qld, 46% Vic., 36% NT, 26% SA, 20% WA, 15% ACT and 7% Tas.

Ecotourism

A large number of international visitors become involved in activities associated with ecotourism. In a 1994 survey of tourists aged 15 years and over, 50% responded that they had visited national or state parks, reserves or caves.

- 13% said they had taken part in a bush walk.
- 11% undertook rainforest walks.
- 12% took part in coral viewing.
- 2% went on outback safari tours.

Employment in the tourism industry

In 1993–94 535 600 persons were employed in the tourism industry: 28.3% in restaurants, hotels and clubs and 21.4% in the retail trade.

- 76% were employed in full-time jobs, including 90% of males and 58% of females.

Tourism forecasts

The Tourism Forecasting Council estimates that to the year 2006 international visitor arrivals will increase at an average rate of 7.8% to reach 8.6 million.

- Real tourism export earnings are estimated to reach $34bn in 2006, an increase of $16bn on 1996.

MINING AND MINERALS

In world terms Australia is the largest exporter of alumina, black coal, diamonds, iron ore, lead and mineral sands products, the second largest exporter of zinc and the third largest exporter of aluminium and gold. In 1994–95 the mining industry contributed $16 889m, or 4% of Australia's GDP.

Employment in the mining industry

In 1995–96, 85 000 people were employed in the mining industry, a decline of 10 000 from the 95 000 employees of 1990–91.

▶ $3590m was paid in wages and salaries in 1994–95, with an industry turnover of $28 936m.

▶ The turnover per employee was $52 282.95.

Private mineral and petroleum exploration expenditure

In 1996–97 a total of $2001.5m was expended on private mineral and petroleum exploration.

▶ $1148.6m was spent on mineral exploration; $251.9m was spent on onshore oil exploration and $601m on offshore oil exploration.

Mining production and exports earnings 1995–96

Total mineral resources exports earned $34 123m in 1995–96, and mineral merchandise earned $75 306m.

Bauxite production and exports

43 308 kt of bauxite was mined, from which 13 326 kt of alumina and 1331 kt of aluminium (ingot metal) was produced. Bauxite exports were worth $85m, alumina $2717m and aluminium (ingot metal) $2379m.

Coal production and exports

243 019 kt of raw black coal, 194 514 kt of black coal and 53 604 kt of brown coal were produced. Exports of black coal were worth $4746m, of coking coal $3014m, and of steaming coal $928m.

Copper production and exports

A total of 483 kt of copper ore was mined, producing 172 kt of blister copper and 293 kt of refined copper. Copper exports were worth $928m.

Diamonds

Mining yielded 42 566 carats of diamonds, from which there were exports of $531m in value.

Gems, other than diamonds
Gems other than diamonds had an export value of $136m.

Gold, refined
317 951 kg of refined gold was produced, earning $5607m.

Iron ore
147 861 kt of iron ore, 7554 kt of pig iron and 8471 kt of raw steel were produced. Exports of ore and pellets brought in $2865m, iron, steel and ferroalloys $1787m.

Lead
505 kt of lead was mined and 181 kt of bullion and 224 kt of refined lead produced. Lead exports earned $456m.

Magnesite
The mining of 307 530 t of magnesite was worth $48m in exports.

Manganese ore and concentrate
2168 t were mined and exports were worth $212m.

Nickel
106 t were mined and exports were worth $1157m.

Petroleum products

Petroleum, field production

crude oil and condensate	30 251 ML
LPG (naturally occurring)	3649 ML
natural gas	29 985 Mm^3

Petroleum, refinery

LPG	1448 ML
automotive gasoline	18 358 ml
aviation turbine fuel	4882 ml
other	5169 ml

Petroleum exports earnings

crude oil and other refinery feed stock	$1675m
LNG	$1372m
LPG	$189m
refinery products	$933m

Salt
Salt production was 8255 kt, with export earnings of $179m.

Silver
1019 t of silver ore were mined from which 350 t were refined; export earnings were $62m.

Tin
Mining production was 9172 t with 550 t refined. Refined tin exports brought in $61m.

Uranium (yellow cake)
5105 t were produced with export earnings of $242m.

Zinc
Mine production was 1035 kt from which 330 kt were refined, with export earnings of $816m.

Zircon concentrate
Production of 496 kt brought in export earnings of $223m.

Mineral royalty receipts by governments
The Commonwealth and state/territory governments received a total of $1 017 518m in mineral royalties in 1994–95, a rise of 2.9% on the previous year.

▶ Qld received the largest amount in royalties, at $301 669m, followed by WA at $287 659m.

CONSTRUCTION INDUSTRY

Residential buildings
The term residential buildings for statistical purposes embraces the construction of dwelling units, e.g. new houses, flats, apartments, villa units, townhouses, duplexes, etc.

Building commencements
122 304 dwelling units were commenced in 1995–96 to a total value of $12 172m. In 1988–89 there were 174 963 commencements with a value of $13 527m.

Price index of materials used in house building
With the reference base year 1989–90 = 100, the price index for materials used in house building was an average 115.7 for the six capital cities, ranging from 115.4 in Melbourne to 120.7 in Hobart.

Non-residential building
There were 11 134 commencements

of non-residential buildings in 1995–96 with a value of $26 079m. The corresponding figures for 1988–89 were 16 056 commencements valued at $14 590m.

Price index of materials used in non-residential building

With the reference base year 1989–90 = 100, the price index for materials used in building, other than house building, was an average of 112.7 for the six capital cities, ranging from 111.1 in Melbourne to 115.1 in Hobart.

Engineering construction

In 1995–96 private sector engineering construction was valued at $7144.2m at average 1989–90 prices, compared with $4963.8m in 1989–90. The total work done by the public sector was $8352.8m in 1995–96 and $7012.4m in 1989–90.

◗ The construction of roads, highways and subdivisions in 1995–96 was the major category of engineering construction, being responsible for $4335m, or 29.7% of the value all engineering work done.

◗ The construction of work associated with electricity generation, transmission and generation was worth $1355m, or 9.28% of the value of engineering construction work done.

THE MEDIA

The print media
Newspapers

On 3 March 1803 Governor King founded Australia's first newspaper, the government-owned *Sydney Gazette and New South Wales Advertiser*. The first privately owned paper published in Australia was the weekly *Australian*, which first appeared on 14 October 1824. The oldest existing Australian newspaper is the *Sydney Morning Herald (SMH)*, which was launched on 18 April 1831.

The 1992 House of Representatives' Select Committee on the Print Media pointed out that the Australian print media industry is highly concentrated, with two groups in a dominant position in the number of publications and related activities. These print media groups also have substantial interests in radio stations and television stations.

- In July 1997 there were three national newspapers (*The Australian*, *The Australian Financial Review* and *The Daily Commercial News*), 20 metropolitan, 158 suburban and 408 regional newspapers.
- There were also 1692 magazines and 275 newsletters.
- In July 1997, the paper with the biggest circulation in Australia was Melbourne's *Herald–Sun*, which produces four editions each day Monday–Friday, with 558 500, followed by Sydney's *Daily Telegraph*, published in the afternoon, with 346 988. Sydney's *Sunday Telegraph* had the biggest circulation of the Sunday papers at 701 651.

The ethnic press

The multicultural composition of the population is reflected in Australia's flourishing ethnic press. As at July 1997, there were 98 newspapers aimed at 36 language groups published, some bi-weekly and others weekly. The Arabic-language

Al Farasha had a circulation of 60 000, the Lebanese *Al Bairak* 36 340, the *Spanish Herald* 35 560 and the Greek *Ellinis* 23 370.

Radio and television broadcasting

The first wireless message transmitted in Australia was at Adelaide in 1899, being sent a distance of 600 yards from the Government Observatory. On 22 September 1918 the first direct wireless message was sent to Australia from the United Kingdom. On February 1926 radio station 2GB (Grace Brothers) commenced broadcasting in Sydney.

▶ In July 1997 there were five national broadcasting services, 107 metropolitan and 110 regional radio stations. There were also 101 non-profiting-making public broadcasting stations.

▶ In 1993–94 there were 19 375 employees in the industry. Radio services had an operating profit before taxes of $17.7m and television services $376.9m.

▶ In 1992 the average time spent listening to the radio as a part of all activities was 101 minutes per day and watching television was 172 minutes per day.

Television broadcasting

The first of Australia's television services went to air on 16 September 1956, almost 20 years after the first screening in London. The first stations were TCN–9 in Sydney and HSV–7 in Melbourne. In Sydney ABC Channel 2 began regular transmission on 5 November 1956.

▶ In July 1997 there were 31 metropolitan and 22 regional TV stations. There were also 10 community TV stations, six of which were in NSW.

▶ There were five subscription TV services and two satellite TV services, one each in NSW and Qld.

▶ In February 1996 3% of households were receiving pay TV.

The Australian Broadcasting Service (ABC)
The ABC radio transmitter network

In 1995–96 the ABC broadcast on 638 transmitters.

	AM	FM
Radio National	21	224
Metropolitan radio	8	2
Regional radio	72	186
ABC Classic FM	–	66
Triple J	–	48
Parliamentary & News Network	8	–
shortwave radio	3	–

▶ In 1995–96 the ABC's average staff level was 5385, compared with 5457 the previous year.

▶ In addition Radio Australia had 16 transmitters. On 1 July 1997 as a cost-cutting measure transmissions in Cantonese ceased and the transmitters at Carnarvon (WA) and Darwin were closed down.

▶ The Homestead and Community Broadcasting Satellite Service allows those living outside transmitter range to receive signals from ABC radio and television. About 12 000 satellite dishes were in service for direct-to-home reception of HACBSS.

The ABC television transmitter service

In 1995–96 the ABC had 614 TV transmitters.

▶ The ABC's program analysis in 1995–96 showed that 54.3% of its programs were Australian-produced.

Special Broadcasting Service (SBS)

In June 1975 the government established experimental ethnic radio stations 2EA and 3EA in Sydney and Melbourne respectively, and in September 1976 the ABC was requested to set up a permanent ethnic broadcasting service. The SBS was established in January 1978 and assumed responsibility for 2EA and 3EA. SBS commenced multicultural television transmission in Sydney and Melbourne in October 1980. The government agreed to allow limited advertising on SBS television and radio in June 1991.

▶ During 1995–96, SBS management had consultations with 69 different cultural communities and the service broadcast programs in 55 languages apart from English.

SBS transmitter service
The SBS delivers its radio programs from stations in Sydney (2EA) and Melbourne (3EA) and through its transmitter network covers all states' and territories' capital cities and regional areas.

▶ The SBS television service covers an area containing at least 15.8 million people and reaches 4.6 million people.

▶ The service has a weekly reach of 23.8% of TV viewers born in Australia, 57.6% of TV viewers born in Europe and 39.3% of TV viewers born in Asia.

▶ SBS TV has a weekly reach of 38.3% of TV viewers aged 40+ years.

COMMUNICATION SERVICES

The communication services industry includes telecommunications, postal and courier services. In 1994–95 there were 1600 operating businesses, a growth of over 300% since 1990–91. Employment in the industry had declined from 127 000 to 124 000 in the same period.

Postal services

On 10 July 1803 the *Sydney Gazette* announced the first mail service within Australia, authorising a charge of twopence for letters between Sydney and Parramatta (NSW). A post office was set up in Sydney on

25 April 1809. A total of 4047.4 million mail articles were handled by Australia Post in 1995–96, compared with 3827.7 million in 1994–95, an increase of 5.43%.

▶ Australia Post had 32 040 full-time employees in 1995–96 compared with 33 605 in 1991–92.

▶ There were 4317 Australia Post outlets, comprising 1132 corporate offices, and 2822 licensed post offices and post office agencies.

Mail delivery network

In 1995–96 there were 7.92 million delivery points: 5.97 million households received their mail by street delivery, 622 722 from private boxes/locked bags, 44 018 by private and community bags, 342 893 by roadside delivery and 155 025 by counter delivery.

▶ 387 436 businesses received their mail by street delivery, 369 078 by way of private boxes/locked bags, 5033 by private and community bags, 12 897 by roadside delivery and 14 656 by counter delivery.

Postal articles handled

In 1994 Australia Post handled a total of 3827.7 million postal articles; the 1990–91 total was 3214.8 million.

▶ Of the 1994–95 total 3529.9 million articles were posted in Australia for delivery in Australia, 146.4 million were posted in Australia for delivery overseas and 151.4 million posted overseas for delivery in Australia.

▶ The on-time letter delivery performance was 93.2%.

Basic postage rate

If the CPI base is taken as 1989–90 = 100 the real cost of a 45c stamp has decreased by –3.1%.

Australia Post finances

In 1995–96 Australia Post had revenue totalling $2915.8m and expenditure of $2517.7m. Its profit before abnormals and tax was $433.1m. A dividend of $143m was paid to the Commonwealth government.

Telecommunication services

Australia's first telegraph service between Melbourne and Williamstown (Vic.) was opened in February 1854. In 1858 intercolonial telegraph lines were established linking Sydney, Melbourne and Adelaide. The Overland Telegraph Line, the first to reach from coast to coast to link Port Augusta (SA) and Darwin, was completed on 22 August 1872. At present there are two licensed general telecommunications carriers in Australia, Telstra and Optus Communications. Telstra is majority-owned by the Commonwealth government while Optus is a publicly listed company.

Telstra 1996–97

Operating revenue totalled $15 983m compared with $15 239m the previous year. There was a profit before tax and abnormals of $3805m, the 1995–96 figure being $3242m. The dividend to the Commonwealth government was $4146m, compared with $3150m in 1995–96.

- In November 1996 the Commonwealth government sold about a third of Telstra to private and corporate shareholders for approximately $14 bn. 60% of shares were bought by public applicants and Telstra employees, and 40% by institutional applicants.
- Telstra's full-time workforce numbered 66 109, down from 76 522 in 1995–96.
- Over 70% of all phone books were recycled during 1995–96 through the national Book Muncher scheme, in excess of double the number in 1992. The 5500 t collected was used for products such as cat litter, egg cartons and housing insulation.
- Telstra's waste copper cable was also recycled, the plastic sheathing being reprocessed as a cover for racecourses, and the copper extracted by smelting.

- By 30 June 1997 there were more than a million digital mobile customers, the broadband network passed 2.1 million houses, and there had been a 20% expansion in digital mobile network geographic coverage.

Optus Communications

Following open-tender bidding, the Commonwealth government selected Optus in November 1991 as the new telecommunications carrier to bring about the benefits of a competitive environment. Optus purchased Aussat (the national satellite owner and carrier), which was licensed as a general private sector competitive carrier, and commenced operations, with telecommunications and mobile carrier licences, on 31 January 1992. Revenue totalled $1944m in 1995–96, a 36% increase over 1994–95, and there was an operating profit before tax of $60m.

- Full-time employees with Optus Communications totalled 4186 in 1995–96.
- As at 30 June 1996 Optus had secured 16% of the national and international long-distance market, 31% of the mobile market and the customer accounts of 57% of the top 500 companies.

Mobile phones

The Commonwealth government has announced its commitment to phase out the Analogue Mobile Phone Service (AMPS) network by 1 January 2000. Digital mobile phone services are progressively replacing the AMPS network.

- In December 1995 there were 2.55 million subscribers to the analogue mobile market, 70.6% being on the Telstra MobileNet and 29.4% being with Optus.
- In July 1996 there were 920 000 subscribers on the digital mobile market, 38% being with Telstra, 38% with Optus and 24% with Vodaphone.

▶ Australia has one of the world's highest penetration rates for mobile phone ownership. More than one in five Australians owns a mobile phone. In February 1996 4.3% of Australian households had a car phone.

Households owning/paying for communications technologies

In February 1996 96.8% of Australian households had telephone connections. The gross product of the communications services industries was $12 400m.

▶ 24.1% of Australian households had answering machines, 24.1% had mobile phones and 13.4% had cordless phones.

▶ 9.2% had facsimile machines (3% on dedicated lines and 5.8% on other connections).

Costs of a telephone call

Although the telecommunications industry has largely been deregulated, Australia has some of the most expensive local and international calls of the developed world.

Cost of a standard 3-minute local call, 1 February 1997– 1 February 1998

	($A)
Australia	**0.230**
Belgium	0.203
United Kingdom	0.203
Germany	0.197
Sweden	0.155
France	0.154
Netherlands	0.127
New Zealand	0.121
Japan	0.117
Italy	0.112

Cost of a standard 3-minute international call, 1 February 1997–1 February 1998

	($A)
Australia	**3.08**
Japan	2.94
Germany	2.86
United States	2.57
Italy	2.38
Belgium	2.33
New Zealand	2.26
Netherlands	2.02
Sweden	2.00
Canada	1.62

INDEX

Aboriginal and Torres Strait Islander peoples, *see* indigenous peoples
aerodromes 215–16
aged care 73–4
agricultural industries 188–9, *see also* fisheries; timber industry
  crops 190–3
  employment 189
  land use 189–90
  livestock 194–6
air transport 215–7
Antarctic Territory 6
Ashmore Islands 6
aviation, *see* aerodromes; air transport

births, *see also* contraception; pregnancy
  adoptions 58
  age-specific birth rates 55–6
  breastfeeding 58
  caesarean 56
  confinements 56
  crude birth rate 53–4
  defects 58
  ex-nuptial 54–5
  fertility rates 54, 55
  IVF and GIFT 57
  marital status of mothers 55
  multiple 57
bushfires 13
businesses
  bankruptcies 186
  company profits before taxes 184
  farm 188–9
  small 184–5, 188

Cartier Islet 6
Christmas Island 6
climate
  drought 8, 9, 10
  flood 10–11
  fog 11
  frost 11
  hail 12
  impact of climate change 12
  rainfall 8, 9–10, 12, 33–4, 83, 84
  snow 11
  temperature 9
  thunder 12
  wind 11–12
Cocos (Keeling) Islands 7
communication services industry 231, *see also* postal services; telecommunications
community services 75
  aged care 74
  child support 73
  expenditure 76
  government involvement 76
  residential facilities 74, 77
  source of income 77
companion animals 27–9
computers 203–4
construction industry 225–6
contraception 57
Coral Sea Islands Territory 7
courts 142
credit card transactions 185
crime
  assaults 136
  burglary 139
  cost of 134, 144
  credit card 140
  drug offences 140
  household 139
  kidnapping/abduction 135
  larceny 139
  motor vehicle theft 139–40
  personal 134–5
  robbery 136
  sexual assault 138
  unlawful killing 135–6, 137
  women's experience of violence 138

cultural sector
  activities
    cinema attendance 146, 151
    dance 148
    music 146, 148
    reading habits 148
    video hiring and watching 151
  books 147–8
  film and video production 150
  funding 149–50
  motion picture exhibition industry 150–1
  occupations 149
  performing arts 148–9
  venues
    art museums 146
    botanical gardens 146, 147
    libraries 146, 147
    marine parks 146, 147
    museums 146–7
    zoological gardens 146, 147

deaths 58, *see also* infant mortality; maternal mortality; poisoning
  accidental 22, 23–4, 30, 62, 210–12
  AIDS-related 60–1
  cancer 60
  childhood diseases 62
  crude death rate 59
  drugs
    illicit 98
    legal 96, 97
  females 59, 60, 61, 64, 96, 97, 98
  homicide 65
  males 59–60, 61, 64, 96, 97, 98
  marital status 59–60
  perinatal 63
  suicide 64
defence 169–70
  civilian personnel 172
  coastal surveillance 48
  expenditure 171–2

involvement in wars 169–71
military equipment 172–3
Office of War Graves 173
service personnel 172
war veterans 173
disabilities, people with 74–5
divorce 67–8, 69
children 69
crude divorce rate 68
domestic animals, *see* companion animals
donations 185
drug abuse, *see also* petrol sniffing
alcohol 96
deaths 96
road crashes 212
taxation 98
illicit drugs
deaths 98
seizures by Australian Customs 98–9
sport 99
tobacco smoking 96–7
deaths 97
household expenditure 97
taxation 97, 98

earthquakes 4
economic indicators
balance of payments 181–2
exchange rates 181, 182
foreign debt 182
price indexes 178–9
education, *see also* schools; vocational education and training (VET)
age of leaving school 112–13
assistance for isolated children (AIC) 113–14
attainment in maths and science 111
attainment of persons aged 15–64 120
AUSTUDY 113
government expenditure 109
government responsibility 108–9
graduates' starting salaries 116
higher 114
age of students 116
enrolment status of students 115
fields of study 115
male/female ratios 114–15
overseas students 118
people with university degrees 120
higher institutions
size by enrolment 116
staffing 116
open learning 116
overseas students 117–18
preschool 109–10
School of the Air 114
secondary 112
Electronic Funds Transfer (EFT) 185
emergency services 12
energy
coal gas 204–5
electricity 205–6
exports 206
household expenditure 204
natural gas 205
environment, *see also* pollution; waste management
attitudes of the people 33
Clean Up Australia Day 38
costs of environmental protection 38
external territories 6–7

families 70–73, *see also* households
fauna 16–17
amphibians 20
birds 20–2
crocodiles 22–3
dolphins 24
dugongs 24–5
extinctions 17
marsupials 17–19
monotremes 19
placental mammals 19
reptiles 22
sharks 23
trade in 25
whales 24
feral animals 25–7
fire services 12–14, *see also* bushfires
firearms 136–7
buyback program 137–8
fisheries 197–9
flora 14
indigenous species 14
threatened species 14
foodstuffs 105
beverages 105–6
household expenditure
food 108
non-alcoholic beverages 108
solid food consumption
butter, table margarine and cheese 106–7
cereals and cereal products 108
eggs and poultry 107
fruit 107
ice cream and related products 108
red meat and meat products 107
seafood 107
sugar and honey 108
vegetables 107–8
forests
exotic 15
farm trees 15
native 15

gambling 154–5
casinos 156
dog racing 155

238 AUSTRALIA IN FACTS AND FIGURES

expenditure 155
horse racing 155
lotteries 155–6
poker machines 156
takings by type 156
taxation 156

geography
  coastline 3
  continental shelf 3
  highest point 3
  islands 2–3, 6–7
  lakes 4
  land area 2
  latitudinal distance 2
  longitudinal distance 2
  lowest point 3
  oceans 2
  rivers 3
  seas 2

government, *see* government finance; parliamentary government

government finance, *see also* taxation
  consolidated outlays 168
  local government 162, 168
  notes and coins on issue 169
  state governments 167–8
  territories finance 167–8

health, *see also* health care services; health expenditure; health insurance
  children 94
    immunisation 62, 94
    infectious diseases 62, 94
    lead in 94
    sun protection 94
  conditions (*see also* drug abuse)
    asthma 93–4
    breast cancer 94, 100
    prostrate cancer 94
  gender differences 95
  general health and wellbeing 95–6

health care services
  ambulance services 92
  employment 91–3
  hospitals 90–1
  pathology services 91–2
  private medical practice industry 91

health expenditure
  bulk-billed 89
  household 89
  patient-billed 89
  percentage of GDP 88
  total 88

health insurance 87
  Medicare 87–8, 89
  private 89–90

Heard Island 7
heritage, *see* National Estate
hospitality/services turnover 184

households 70
  lone-person 71

housing
  change of residence 84
  community 86–7
  dwellings
    problems 85
    structure 82
    types and number of rooms 84
  finance
    affordability 85
    bank loan rates 83
    commitments on housing 185
    expenditure on mortgage payments 84
    prices, monthly median 85
  private dwellings
    being purchased 82, 83
    fully owned 82, 83
    rented 82, 83
  public rental 86–7

immigration 45–6
  age of immigrants 46, 47
  arrivals 46
  boat people 48
  citizenship 50
  country of birth 49
  eligibility categories 47
  overstayers 48
  sex of overseas born 47

immunisation 62

indigenous peoples 52
  aged-care recipients 74
  breastfeeding 58
  children in supported placements 73
  death
    causes 99–100
    in custody 133–4
    rates 53
  defence force personnel 172
  drug abuse 99
  education 116, 117
    ABSTUDY 113
  elected representatives 163
  fertility rates 53
  health 99, 100
  housing 85–6
  infant birth weight 57
  infant mortality 63
  land purchases 53
  languages 79–81
  law and justice 132–3
  population 40, 52–3
  racial discrimination 51–2
  religions 77–8

industrial disputes 131–2

infant mortality 62–3
  perinatal deaths 63
  Sudden Infant Death Syndrome (SIDS) 64

inflation 178

insect pests 29–30

investment
  Australian overseas 183–4
  foreign in Australia 183, 184

irrigation
  area 33
  Murray–Darling Basin 3

land degradation
  erosion 4–5
  native vegetation loss 5
  production lost 3–4
  salinity 5
  soils 5, 33
land utilisation
  fertiliser use 33
  irrigation 3, 33
languages
  indigenous 79–81
  non-English 81–2
  proficiency in English 82
  self-rating skills 80, 81
life expectancy 43
local government 162–3, 168

manufacturing 188, 199–200
  employment 200, 201
  gross product 200
  sales 200
  trading profit 200
marriage
  age at marriage 65–6
  category of marriage
    celebrants 66–7
  de facto 67
  rate 65, 66, 67
  remarriages 66
maternal mortality 63–4
McDonald Island 7
media, *see* newspapers; radio
  broadcasting; television
  broadcasting
migration
  internal 50–1
  overseas 43, 45
mineral exploration expenditure 223
mineral royalty receipts 225
mining industry 222–5
monorail services 215
motor vehicles 209–10, *see also* road crashes
Murray–Darling Basin

agricultural production 3
area 3
rainfall changes predicted 12

National Estate
  aboriginal sites 30
  heritage sites 30–1
  national trusts 32–3
  nature conservation reserves 31
  places lost 31
  World Heritage Listings 32
newspapers 228
  ethnic press 228–9
Norfolk Island 7

organ donation 65
overseas aid program 173–5
overseas visitors 41

parliamentary government, *see also* local government
  Commonwealth
    House of Representatives 160
    Senate 159–60
  elections 161–2
    funding for political parties 161
  referendums 160–1
  state 162
  structure 158
  voting 158–9
pensions, *see* social security
people with disabilities 74–5
petrol sniffing 99
petroleum 223–4
pharmaceutical benefits 92–93
pharmaceuticals
  cost 93
  most prescribed drug 93
pharmacies 92–3
poisoning 64
police 140–1
  expenditure 141

  gender 141, 142
  people shot by 141–2
  public relations 142
  salaries 141
  size of forces 141
  work and health 141
pollution
  air 35–6
  waterways 36
population, *see also* immigration
  age distribution 42, 73–4
  density 42
  emigration 43, 50
  geographical distribution 40, 44, 50–1
  growth 41, 43, 45
    immigration 45–7
    projected 41, 74
    regional 44
    states and territories 41
  life expectancy 43
  sex distribution 42
  turnover 45
postal services 231–2
poverty 105
pregnancy
  contraception 57
  terminations 57
prisons 142–3
  Australians in foreign 144–5
  costs of public 145
  deaths 133–4, 145
  escapes 145
  juvenile corrective institutions 144
  prisoner numbers 143–4
  private 143
public safety and order 145

racial discrimination 51–2
radio broadcasting 229
  Australian Broadcasting Service (ABC) 230
  Special Broadcasting Service (SBS) 230–1

railways 212
  commuters 213
  disasters 213
  employed persons 214
  level-crossing accidents 213–14
  non-government 213
recreation
  fishing 145–6
  household expenditure 146
  national parks 145
religions
  Christian 78–9
  indigenous peoples 77–8
  non-Christian 79
research and development 202
  business expenditure (BERD) 202–3
  higher education expenditure (HERD) 203
retail trade 184
retirement 73–4
road crashes 210–11
  cost of 212
  fatalities 24, 62, 211–12
  hospitalisation 212
road transport 208, *see also* motor vehicles; road crashes
  travel to work 210

salt 224
schools
  government
    fees 111
    numbers 110
    staffing 111
    students attending 110
  non-government
    fees 111
    numbers 110
    staffing 111
    students attending 110
  primary
    attendance 110
    staffing 111
    student enrolment 110
  secondary
    attendance 110, 112
    staffing 111
service industries 188, 204
  hospitality/services turnover 184
shipping 207–8
  coastal 208
  maritime safety 208
social security
  Family Payment 102
  pensions
    age 101, 102
    disability 101, 102
    sole parents 101, 102
    war widow 101
  sickness payments 102
  unemployment allowances 129–30
  Youth Allowance 102–3
sport
  attendance 153–4
  expenditure
    government 152
    personal 152
  injuries 153
  most expensive activities 152
  most popular activities 152
  participation 151–2
    children 152–3
sports industries
  employment and volunteers 154
  financial operations 154
  operations 154
standard times 7
state government 162, 167–8
stock market indexes 182–3
superannuation 103
  contributions 104
  persons covered 103–4
  persons not covered 104
  retirement payment arrangements 104

superannuation funds 104–5

taxation 163
  average taxable income 167
  Capital Gains Tax (CGT) 165
  Commonwealth government 164
  evasion 166
  Fringe Benefits Tax (FBT) 165
  income tax on enterprises 165
  income tax on non-residents 165
  late lodgement of returns 167
  local government 165
  PAYE system 165
  per head of population 163
  personal income 165
  prosecutions 166
  revenue 163–4, 166
    refunds 165
  sales tax and excises 165
telecommunications 233
  households
    communications technologies 235
    telephone connections 235
  mobile phones 234–5
  Optus Communications 234
  telephone call costs 235
  Telstra 233–4
television broadcasting 229–30
  Australian Broadcasting Service (ABC) 230
  Special Broadcasting Service (SBS) 230–1
textiles, clothing and footwear (TCF) 201
  employment 201–2
  homeworking 202
timber industry 196–7
time zones 7
tourism 218
  accommodation 221
  and koalas 219
  backpackers 222

domestic 220
ecotourism 222
employment 222
expenditure by Australian residents 220–1
expenditure by overseas visitors 219
forecasts 222
inbound international 218
outward bound 220
regions visited by overseas tourists 219
trade
 balance of payments 181–2
 exports 179–80, 182
 imports 180, 182
trade unions 130
 casual employees 131
 female membership 131
 industry representation 131
 number 131
 permanent employees 131
tramways 214–15
transport, *see also* railways; road transport; shipping
 household expenditure 210

unemployment
 duration in weeks 128
 income support 129–30
 job search experience 129
 long-term 128
 rate 128

vocational education and training (VET) 118–19
 apprentices 119
 clients 119, 120
 employer-based training 119
 TAFE 119

waste management 36–8
 sewage 34, 35
water
 household consumption 83–4
 supplies 3, 33–5
weeds 15–16
wildlife, *see* fauna
workforce, *see also* unemployment
 adults not in 129
 average weekly earnings 124–5
 employed persons
  by industry 122
  by occupation 122
  parents 72
 employment levels by occupation group 126
 females 120–1, 122, 123, 124
 full-time 122, 123
 hours of work 123
 household income 126
 job vacancies 126–7
 labour costs 127
 males 122–3, 124
 overtime 123–4
 part-time 123
  involuntary 129
 participation rate 121
 people with disabilities 75
 personal income 125–6
 private sector 122
 public sector 122, 128
 status in employment 121
 volunteers 130
 work at home 124
 worker satisfaction with management 127